M000105677

The Oratorio Anthology

Baritone/Bass

Compiled and Edited by Richard Walters

Assistant Editors: Elaine Schmidt, Laura Ward
Repertoire Consultant: David Berger
Historical Consultant: Virginia Saya

On the cover: André Derain, French, *The Last Supper*, oil on canvas, 1911, 226.7 x 288.3 cm, Gift of Mrs. Frank R. Lillie, 1946.339. © 1993, The Art Institute of Chicago, All Rights Reserved.

ISBN 978-0-7935-2508-9

7777 W. Bluemound Rd. P.O. Box 13819 Milwaukee, WI 53213

Contents

Notes and Translations

Carl Philipp Emanuel Bach
1714-1788

MAGNIFICAT
1750
text taken from Luke 1:46-55, from the Vulgate (the 4th century, authorized Roman Catholic Latin translation of the Bible); besides these verses a Magnificat (the canticle of the Virgin) traditionally includes two additional verses of the Lesser Doxology "Gloria Patri et Filio"

Composed 1749. Possibly first performed 1750, at Thomaskirche, Leipzig. The trumpet, timpani, and horn parts were added later to the original scoring.

Fecit potentiam

Fecit potentiam in brachio suo: dispersit superbos mente cordis sui.	*He has shown the might of his arm:* *he scatters those with proud minds from one another.*

Johann Sebastian Bach
1685-1750

MAGNIFICAT
BWV 243a and 243
1723
text taken from Luke 1:46-55, from the Vulgate (the 4th century, authorized Roman Catholic Latin translation of the Bible); besides these verses a Magnificat (the canticle of the Virgin) traditionally includes two additional verses of the Lesser Doxology "Gloria Patri et Filio"

Composed for Bach's first Christmas in Leipzig. It was later revised (c1728-1731) and transposed from E-flat to D. The revision replaces recorders with flutes and omits 4 interpolated hymns (laudes), which had previously rendered the text appropriate to the Christmas season. The revised Magnificat was possibly first performed July 2, 1733 for the Feast of the Visitation of Mary. The Magnificat was sung in German for Sunday vespers, and in Latin on Christmas Day.

Quia fecit mihi magna

The aria is scored for continuo.

Quia fecit mihi magna qui potens est et sanctum nomen ejus.	*For he to me is mighty who has done great things* *and holy is his name.*

Dates throughout are for first performances unless otherwise noted. The bracketed aria titles are those used when performing the singing English translation found in the musical score. The notes in this section are by the editor.

MASS IN B MINOR

composed 1724-1740s
text is the traditional Latin Mass from the Roman Catholic liturgy

Not initially conceived as a unity, the different sections of what would eventually be the Mass in B minor were composed over a period of perhaps as much as 25 years. The Sanctus was composed in 1724 and first performed on Christmas Day in that year at Thomaskirche, Leipzig. The Kyrie and Gloria sections, comprising what was then known as the Missa in Lutheran terminology, were composed and first performed in 1733, probably in Dresden. At some later point Bach composed the remaining sections with the result of a complete traditional mass. The sources are unclear, and there is disagreement about the dates of composition for the Credo, Osanna, Benedictus, Agnus Dei, and Dona nobis pacem. Among the new composition there was some significant borrowing of music from earlier works. Bach's work to complete the mass was probably done in the 1740s, with theories that put it as late as 1748 or 1749, which would make the Mass in B minor perhaps the composer's last major composition. (*The Art of the Fugue* was probably principally composed early in the decade.) Earlier historical theories stated that these remaining sections were composed at different times, primarily in the 1730s, and that Bach assembled the mass into a whole near the end of his life. The first performance of the complete work was in 1859 in Leipzig.

Et in Spiritum sanctum

From the Credo section, scored for 2 oboe d'amores and continuo.

Et in Spiritum sanctum	*And in the Holy Spirit*
Dominum et vivificantem,	*Lord and giver of life,*
qui ex Patre Filioque procedit;	*who from the Father as a Son proceeds;*
qui cum Patre et Filio simul	*who with the Father and the Son together*
adoratur et conglorificatur;	*is adored and glorified;*
qui locutus est per Prophetas.	*who spoke by the prophets.*
Et unam sanctam catholicam	*And one holy catholic*
et apostolicam ecclesiam.	*and apostolic church.*

PASSIO SECUNDUM JOANNEM

(Johannes-Passion/St. John Passion)
BWV 245
1724
libretto based primarily on *Der für die Sünden der Welt gemarterte und sterbende Jesus* (Jesus tortured and dying for the sins of the world) by Barthold Heinrich Brockes (1712), with some additional free texts from a 1704 Passion libretto by Christian Heinrich Postel (free text refers to poetry that is not an adaptation or paraphrase of Scripture), with adaptations and additional material by the composer

Composed in 1723, the Passion was first performed on Good Friday, April 7, 1724 at Thomaskirche, Leipzig. The piece was revised, with additions, deletions and substitutions, for performances in 1725, but basically restored to the original version for performances in c1730 and 1740. A Passion is a musical setting of Jesus' sufferings and death as related by one of the four Gospel writers. Brockes' libretto, cited above, was the most often set of Passion librettos by composers in the 18th century.

Betrachte, meine Seel' ***[Consider, O my soul]***

From Part II (no. 31), scored for 2 viole d'amore, lute, bassoon and continuo. This is a free text from Brockes' libretto. The aria was replaced with "Ach, windet euch nicht so" in the 1725 revision.

Betrachte, meine Seel'	*Consider, my soul,*
mit ängstlichem Vergnügen,	*with anxious willingness,*
mit bitt'rer Lust	*with sharp desire*
und halb beklemmt von Herzen,	*and half consticted heart,*
dein höchstes Gut	*your highest blessing*
in Jesu Schmerzen,	*in Jesus' pains,*
wie dir auf Dornen, so ihn stechen,	*for you from the thorns that pierce him,*
die Himmelsschlüsselblumen blüh'n,	*the heavenly flowers bloom!*
du kannst viel süsse Frucht	*you can much sweet fruit*
von seiner Wermut brechen,	*from his wormwood pluck,*
drum sieh ohn Unterlass auf Ihn!	*therefore look without ceasing upon Him!*

PASSIO SECUNDUM MATTHÆUM

(Matthäus-Passion/St. Matthew Passion)
BWV 244
1727 or 1729
libretto by Picander, a pseudonym for Christian Friedrich Henrici (1700-1764); it is probable that the free text poems only were by Henrici (free text refers to poetry that is not a paraphrase or adaptation directly from Scripture), with adapted biblical narrative from the Gospel of Matthew and some chorale texts by the composer

The date of first performance of the Passion is in dispute, occuring at Thomaskirche, Leipzig, on either April 11, 1727 or April 15, 1729. A revised version was performed March 30, 1736. A Passion is a musical setting of Jesus' sufferings and death as related by one of the four Gospel writers.

Gerne will ich mich bequemen	*[**Gladly would I be enduring**]*

From Part I (nos. 28-29), scored for strings and continuo. The aria is a free text of Jesus in the Garden of Gethsemane.

Der Heiland fällt vor seinem Vater nieder, dadurch erhebt er mich und alle von unserm Falle hinauf zu Gottes Gnade wieder. Er ist bereit, den Kelch, des Todes Bitterkeit zu trinken, in welchen Sünden dieser Welt gegossen sind und hässlich stinken, weil es dem lieben Gott gefällt.	*The Savior falls low before the Father,* *thereby to raise me and all of us fallen people* *up to God's grace again.* *He is prepared, the cup* *of death's bitterness to drink,* *in which the sins of this world are poured* *and hideously stinks,* *because the loving God willed it.*
Gerne will ich mich bequemen Kreuz und Becher anzunehmen, trink ich doch dem Heiland nach. Denn sein Mund, der mit Milch und Honig fliesset, hat den Grund und des Leidens herbe Schmach durch den ersten Trunk versüsset.	*Gladly will I submit* *cross and chalice to partake,* *drink I as the Saviour did.* *By his mouth* *which with milk and honey flows,* *has earth and its sorrow's* *harsh humiliation* *through the first drink sweetened.*

Komm, süsses Kreuz	*[**Come, healing cross**]*

From Part II (nos. 65-66). The recitative is scored for flutes, gamba, and continuo; the aria is scored for gamba and continuo. A free text, commenting on the procession as Simon of Cyrene carries the cross for Jesus.

Ja! freilich will in uns das Fleisch und Blut zum Kreuz gezwungen sein; je mehr es unsrer Seele gut, je herber geht es ein.	*Yes! certainly will* *in us the flesh and blood* *to the cross be compelled;* *as more it for our soul is good,* *so harsher goes it for one.*
Komm, süsses Kreuz, so will ich sagen, mein Jesu, gib es immer her! Wird mir mein Leiden einst zu schwer, so hilf du mir es selber tragen.	*Come, sweet cross,* *so will I say,* *my Jesus,* *give it always to me!* *If my sorrow becomes too difficult for me,* *then you will help me to bear it.*

Mache dich, mein Herze, rein *[Make thee clean, my heart]*

From Part II (nos. 74-75). The recitative is scored for strings and continuo; the aria is scored for strings, oboe da caccia, and continuo. Both recitative and aria are free texts, coming just after the death of Jesus in the Passion.

Am Abend, da es kühle war,	*On the evening when it was cool,*
ward Admas Fallen offenbar.	*was Adam's fall manifest;*
am Abend drücket ihn der Heiland nieder;	*on the evening he pushed the Savior low;*
am Abend kam die Taube wieder	*on the evening came the dove again*
und trug ein Oelblatt in dem Munde.	*and bore and olive leaf in its mouth.*
O schöne Zeit! O Abendstunde!	*O beautiful time! O evening hour!*
Der Friedensschluss ist nun mit Gott gemacht,	*the key to peace is only made with God,*
denn Jesus hat sein Kreuz vollbracht.	*because Jesus has His cross endured.*
Sein Leichnam kommt zur Ruh.	*His corpse came to rest.*
Ach, liebe Seele, bitte du, geh,	*O, beloved soul, ask you, go,*
lasse dir den toten Jesum schenken,	*allow you the dead Jesus to bestow,*
o heilsames, o köstlich's Angedenken!	*o healing, o blessed memory!*
Mache dich, mein Herze, rein,	*Make you, my heart, pure,*
ich will Jesum selbst begraben,	*I will Jesus in myself entomb,*
denn er soll nunmehr	*then he shall henceforth*
in mir für und für	*in me for eternity*
seine süsse Ruhe haben.	*his sweet rest have.*
Welt, geh aus, lass Jesum ein!	*World, go out, allow Jesus in!*

WEIHNACHTS-ORATORIUM

(Christmas Oratorio)
BWV 248
1734-1735
text attributed to Picander, a pseudonym for Christian Friedrich Henrici (1700-1764); based on Luke 2:1, 3-12, and Matthew 1:1-12 (the Luther German Bible)

The Weihnachts-Oratorium is actually a collection of six individual church cantatas, designed to be performed at each of the six church events between Christmas and Epiphany. The piece contains newly composed music, and adaptations from three secular cantatas (BWV 213-215). The first cantata was first performed on Christmas Day, 1734 at Thomaskirche, Leipzig. The remaining cantatas followed in order on the second and third days following Christmas, on New Year's Day (Feast of the Circumcision), on the Sunday after New Year, and on the Feast of the Epiphany. Performances took place at both Thomaskirche and Nikolaikirche, Leipzig.

Grosser Herr und starker König *[Mighty Lord and King all glorious]*

From Part I (the first cantata), Christmas Day. Scored for trumpet, flute, strings, continuo.

Grosser Herr, und starker König,	*Great Lord, o mighty king,*
liebster Heiland	*beloved Savior*
o wie wenig achtest du der Erden Pracht!	*o how little do you regard earthly splendor!*
Der die ganze Welt erhält,	*He who preserves the entire world,*
ihre Pracht und Zier er schaffen,	*its splendor and decoration created,*
muss in harten Krippen schlafen.	*must in a rough manger sleep.*

Hector Berlioz
1803-1869

L'ENFANCE DU CHRIST
(The Childhood of Christ)
Opus 25
1854
libretto by the composer, based on the Matthew 2, augmented by legend and invention

Composed 1850-1854. The composer called the piece a *trilogie sacrée* (sacred trilogy). Part I, "Le songe d'Hérode" (Herod's Dream), was composed in 1854. Part II, "La fuite en Egypte" (The Flight into Egypt), was composed 1850, revised 1852. This section was premiered in 1850 under the pseudonym of Pierre Ducré, which Berlioz claimed was a prank. When published in 1852, this section was cited as being "attributed to Pierre Ducré, imaginary chapel master." Part III, "L'arrivée à Saïs" (The Arrival at Sais), was composed in 1853. The story, based on a skeletal biblical foundation from Matthew 2, is of Herod and his pursuit of the infant Jesus, and the holy family's flight into Egypt. The score contains stage directions explaining the events portrayed.

O misère des rois!

The aria, from Part I, is sung by the bass role of Herod, alone at night in his palace, restless and frightful over a dream he has had. Herod's dream is an invention by Berlioz, and not mentioned in Scripture.

Toujours ce rêve!	*Always this dream!*
encore cet enfant	*again that child*
Qui doit me détrôner!	*who can dethrone me!*
Et ne savoir que croire	*And only to be able to believe*
De ce présage menaçant	*this menacing omen*
Pour ma vie et ma gloire!	*for my life and my glory!*
O misère des rois!	*O misery of kings!*
Régner et ne pas vivre!	*To reign and not to live!*
A tous donner des lois,	*To give up all leisure*
Et désirer de suivre	*and to desire to follow*
Le chevrier au fond des bois!	*the goatherd after all through the forest!*
O nuit profonde	*O dead of night*
Qui tiens le monde	*who your people*
Dans le repos plongé,	*into rest plunge,*
A mon sein ravagé	*to my ravaged breast*
Donne la paix une heure,	*give one hour of peace,*
Et que ton voile effleure	*and if your veil brushes*
Mon front d'ennuis chargé!	*my brow between responsibilities!*
Effort stérile!	*Sterile effort!*
Le sommeil fuit;	*The escape of sleep;*
Et ma plainte inutile	*and my useless lamentation*
Ne hâte point ton cours,	*hurries not your course,*
Interminable nuit!	*endless night!*

Gabriel Fauré
1845-1924

REQUIEM
Opus 48
1888
text from the traditional Latin Requiem Mass of the Roman Catholic liturgy; Requiem ("rest") is a Mass for the dead

The manuscript is dated 1887. First performance at the Church of the Madeleine, Paris, January 16, 1888. Revisions and additions made 1887-1890 and in 1893. The first version (scored for violas, cellos, basses, harp, timpani, organ, and violin solo) included a boy choir and boy soloist, and consisted of five movements: Introit et Kyrie, Sanctus, Pie Jesu, Agnus Dei, and In Paradisum. The 1893 version adds the Offertoire and Libera me and includes adult soloists and brass. The 1900 revision and orchestration expands to full orchestra, adding more strings as well as woodwinds. Fauré's Requiem does not conform to the liturgical requirements of the Roman Catholic Church. The Dies Irae is omitted, except for the last two lines, which appear as the Pie Jesu.

Hostias

Hostias et preces Tibi
Domine Laudis offerimus
ta suscipe pro animabus illis
quarum hodie memoriam facimus,
fac eas Domine
de morte transire ad vitam
quam olim Abrahae promisisti
et semini ejus.

Sacrifice and prayer to you
Lord in praise we offer
receive them for the souls
who this day we remember,
grant oh Lord
that they from death pass to life
as it was to Abraham promised
and to his seed.

George Frideric Handel
1685-1759

ALEXANDER'S FEAST
1736
libretto by Newburgh Hamilton, adapted from John Dryden's "Second Ode to St. Cecilia," and also includes sections of Hamilton's earlier work "The Power of Music"

First performed February 19, 1736, London. Revisions in 1737, 1739, 1742, 1751, 1753, and 1755. The character of Timotheus is a minstrel who sings stories to King Alexander; these stories comprise the bulk of the narrative for the oratorio, the theme of which is to show the power of music.

Revenge, Timotheus cries

BELSHAZZAR
1745
libretto by Charles Jennens, based on Daniel 5, Jeremiah 19, Isaiah 44-45, and history

Composed August - September, 1744, and first performed in London March 27, 1745, King's Theatre, Haymarket. The story is during the reign of Belshazzar, king of Babylon, and his defeat by Cyrus, leading to the release of the Jewish captives, including the prophet Daniel.

Behold the monstrous human beast

From Act I, scene 2. Gobrias, a Babylonian, describes the feast of Sesach, where Belshazzar and his court indulge in drunkeness. Because the bass in this role was not up to the aria's vocal demands, it was transposed for a tenor for the first performance.

JOSHUA

1748

libretto by Thomas Morell (1703-1784), based on the book of Joshua

Composed July and August, 1747. First performance took place March 9, 1748 at the Theatre Royal at Covent Garden, London. The oratorio tells the story of the Jewish conquest of Canaan under the leadership of Joshua.

See the raging flames arise

From Act II. Caleb describes the scene after the walls of Jericho have collapsed.

JUDAS MACCABÆUS

1747

libretto by Thomas Morell (1703-1784), based on the book of the Maccabees and the twelfth book of Josephus' *Antiquities of the Jews*

Commissioned by Frederic, Prince of Wales. First performed at the Theatre Royal at Covent Garden, London, April 1, 1747. Revisions and additions were made for frequent new productions, in 1748, then annually from 1750, through 1759. The oratorio relates the restoration of liberty to the Jews under leader Judas Maccabæus.

Arm, arm, ye brave!

From Act I. Simon is inspired by God to choose his brother as the new leader of the Israelites

MESSIAH

1742

text by Charles Jennens (1700-1773), drawn from various biblical sources and the Prayer Book Psalter

Composed between August 22 and September 12, 1741. First performed April 13, 1742 at the Music Hall on Fishamble Street, Dublin. The performance was a benefit for several of the city's charities. The libretto is drawn from the Prophets, the Gospels, the Pauline Epistles, and Revelation, detailing the prophecy of Christ's coming, his life, death resurrection, promise of second coming, and the response of believers. *Messiah* is theological in nature, not the more common dramatic Handelian oratorio. The soloists are impersonal, and the chorus assumes an expanded role as commentators. Many changes and additions were made in the oratorio, with 13 revisions of the score in the years 1743-1759. Many of the solo movements were sometimes sung by different voice types in different versions and keys, a practice the composer directed.

Thus saith the Lord; But who may abide

From Part I. The text is based on Malachi 3:2. The aria is presented in the original version for bass in this anthology edition, which does not contain the familiar *prestissimo* middle section (added in a later version for the castrato alto Gaetano Guadagni).

For behold, darkness shall cover the earth; The people that walked in darkness

From Part I. The recitative text comes from Isaiah 9:2-3. The aria text is based on Isaiah 9:2.

Why do the nations

From Part II. The text comes from Psalm 11:1-2. The aria is presented in its original form, which has become the standard version. Handel later abridged the aria by about half, with a recitative ending, apparently to accommodate an inadequate singer.

The trumpet shall sound

From Part III. The text for the recitative is taken from I Corinthians 15:51-52. The aria's text comes from verses 52 and 53 of the same chapter.

SAMSON
1743
libretto adapted by Newburgh Hamilton from Milton's *Samson Agonistes* and other poems

Composed 1741. First performed February 18, 1743, at the Theatre Royal at Covent Garden, London. Additions and revisions were made for performances in 1745 and 1754. The oratorio relates the story from Judges, with the addition of the character of Micah.

Thy glorious deeds inspir'd my tongue

From Act I. Manoa, Samson's father, recalls his son's military accomplishments and laments Samson's sins.

Honor and arms

From Act II, scene 4. The character of the Philistine Harapha boasts that fighting the blinded Samson is beneath him ("so mean a triumph I disdain").

Franz Joseph Haydn
1732-1809

DIE JAHRESZEITEN
(The Seasons)
1801
libretto by Baron Gottfried van Swieten after "The Seasons," a lengthy pastoral poem by James Thomson, translated into German by Barthold Heinrich Brockes

Begun in 1799, the oratorio was first performed May 20, 1801. Under Haydn's direction and consent, a singing English translation by Swieten (adapting the original poem by Thomson) was included in the first edition of the oratorio, published in 1802 by Breikopf & Härtel. (A German-French edition was also released at the same time.) The first aria below is from Spring, the second from Winter.

Schon eilet froh der Akkermann	***[With joy th'impatient husbandman]***
Vom Widder strahlet jetzt die helle Sonn auf uns herab. Nun weichen Frost und Dampf und schweben laue Dünst umher; der Erde Busen ist gelöst; erhheitert ist die Luft.	*From Aries beams now the shining sun down on us. Now gentle frost and mist and lukewarm vapors float about; the earth's bosom is freed; brighter is the air.*
Schon eilet froh der Ackermann zur Arbeit auf das Feld, in langen Furchen schreitet er dem Pfluge flötend nach. In abgemessnem Gange dann wirft er den Samen aus, den birgt der Akker treu und reift ihn bald zur gold'nen Frucht.	*Already hurries joyful the husbandman to work in the field, in long furrows he strides whistling behind the plow. In measured motion then throws he the seeds out, is sheltered by the faithful earth and ripens soon to golden harvest.*

Erblikke hier, betörter Mensch

Vom dürren Osten dringt
ein scharfer Eishauch jetzt hervor.
Schneidend fährt er durch die Luft,
verzehret jeden Dunst
und hascht des Tieres Odem selbst.
Des grimmigen Tyranns,
des Winters Sieg ist nun vollbracht
und stummer Schrecken drückt
den ganzen Umfang der Natur.

Erblicke hier, betörter Mensch,
erblicke deines Lebens Bild!
Verblühet ist dein kurzer Lenz,
erschöpfet deines Sommers Kraft.
Schon welkt dein Herbst dem Alter zu,
schon naht der bleiche Winter sich
und zeiget dir das offne Grab.
Wo sind sie nun, die hoh'n Entwürfe,
die Hoffnungen vom Glück,
die Sucht nach eitlem Ruhme,
der Sorgen schwere Last?
Wo sind sie nun, die Wonnetage,
verschwelgt in Üppigkeit?
Und wo die frohen Nächte,
im Tauel durchgewacht?
Wo sind sie nun? wo?
Verschwunden sind sie wie ein Traum.
Nur Tugend bleibt.
Die bleibt allein
und leitet uns, unwandelbar,
durch Zeit und Jahreswechsel,
durch Jammer oder Freude
bis zu dem höchsten Ziele hin.

[In this, O vain, misguided man]

From the parched east presses forth
a sharp icy gale now.
It travels cutting through the air,
consumes every vapor
and seizes the animals' breath.
The tyrant's fury,
winter's conquest is now completed
and silent terror afflicts
the whole sphere of nature.

Behold here, deluded man,
behold your life's image!
Bleeding to death is your short spring,
drained your summer's strength.
Already withered of age is your autumn harvest
already the pale winter nears you
and exhibits your open grave.
Where are they now, the high plans,
the hopes for prosperity,
the longing after conceited fame,
sorrow's heavy burden?
Where are they now, the delightful days,
indulged in luxury?
And where the joyful nights
in giddiness awake all night?
Where are they now? Where?
Hazy are they like a dream.
Only virtue remains.
It remains alone
and leads us away unchanging,
through time and the years' changes,
through misery or joy
until we reach the highest destination.

DIE SCHÖPFUNG
Ein Oratorium für jeden Geschmack und jede Zeit
THE CREATION
An Oratorio for All Tastes and Times
1798
libretto attributed to T. Linley or Lidley (sources are unclear about his name), translated from the original English to German and abridged by Baron Gottfried van Swieten, based on chapters from Genesis, selected Psalms, and paraphrases of Milton's *Paradise Lost*

Composition began in 1796. A first, private performance of the oratorio was given April 30, 1798 at the Schwartzenberg Palais (preceded by an open rehearsal April 29). The first public performance was given March 19, 1799. Haydn composed the piece in German, but the English version followed quickly, being basically the original libretto adapted by Swieten. (One of the primary manuscript scores used by Haydn to conduct has both German and English.) English was included in the first published edition, 1800. Since it was the composer's intention that the piece be heard in English in English-speaking countries, in the editor's opinion that is the appropriate language in those locales.

In 1801 Haydn composed a Mass in B-flat that is known as *Schöpfungmesse* (Creation Mass), but this piece is entirely different from the oratorio *Die Schöpfung*. (In the "qui tollis" of the mass Haydn quotes from the oratorio *Die Schöpfung.)*

Rollend in schäumenden Wellen *[Rolling in foaming billows]*

Und Gott sprach:
Es sammle sich das Wasser
unter dem Himmel zusammen an einem Platz,
und es erscheine das trockne Land;
und es war so.
Und Gott nannte das trockne Land:
Erde, und die Sammlung
der Wasser nannte er Meer,
und Gott sah, und es gut war.

And God spoke:
Collect the water
under heaven together in one place,
and let the dry land appear;
and it was so.
And God called the dry land:
Earth, and the collection
of the water he called sea,
and God saw, and it was good.

Rollend in schäumenden Wellen
bewegt sich ungestüm das Meer.
Hügel und Felsen erscheinen der Berge
Gipfel steigt empor.
Der Fläche, weit gedehnt,
durchläuft der breite
Strom in mancher Krümme.
Leise rauschend gleitet fort
im stillen Thal der helle Bach.

Rolling in foaming waves
agitates the turbulent sea.
Hills and rocks appear as the mountain
peaks rise up.
Through the plains, stretched wide,
runs the broad
river with many windings.
Gently rushing glides away
through silent fields the clear brook.

Nun scheint in vollem Glanze der Himmel *[Now heaven in fullest glory shown]*

Gleich öffnet sich der Erde Schoss,
und sie gebiert auf Gottes Wort
Geschöpfe jeder Art, in vollem Wuchs
und ohne Zahl.
Vor Freude brüllend steht der Löwer da.
Hier schiesst der gelenkige Tiger empor.
Das zack'ge Haupt erhebt
der schnelle Hirsch.
Mit fliegender Mähne springt und wieh'rt
voll Mut und Kraft das edle Ross.
Auf grünen Matten weidet schon das Rind,
in Heerden abgetheilt.
Die Triften deckt als wie gesät,
das wollenreiche, sanfte Schaaf.
Wie Staub verbreitet sich
im Schwarm und Wirbel
das Heer der Insekten.
In langen Zügen kriecht
am Boden das Gewürm.

As though opening the earth's womb
and bears God's Word
creatures of every kind in full growth
and without number.
Roaring with joy stands the lion there.
Here leaps the supple tiger upwards.
The jagged head of the
the swift stag raises up.
With flowing mane springs and neights
the noble horse full of courage and strength.
In green alpine meadows graze the cows,
in herds distributed.
The pastures are covered as it is said
with the wooly, gentle sheep.
Like dust spreads itself
in swarm and whirl
the host of insects.
In long processions crawl
on the ground the worms.

Nun scheint in vollem Glanze der Himmel.
Nun prangt in ihrem Schmucke die Erde.
Die Luft erfüllt das leichte Gefieder,
die Wasser schwellt der Fische Gewimmel;
der Boden drückt der Tiere Last.
Doch war noch Alles nicht vollbracht
Dem Ganzen fehlte das Geschöpf,
das Gottes Werke dankbar seh'n,
des herren Gute preisen soll.

Now shines in fullest splendor the heaven.
Now is the earth resplendant in its decoration.
The air is full of light plumage,
the water swells with swarming fish;
the ground is trod by the animals' weight.
However was not all complete.
It lacks the creature,
who God's work grateful sees,
who the Lord's goodness shall praise.

Felix Mendelssohn
1809-1847

ELIJAH
(Elias)
Opus 70
1846
libretto by Julius Schubring, after I Kings 17-19, II Kings 2, and other biblical passages; English libretto by William Bartholomew

Composed summer of 1846. First performed August 26, 1846, at the Birmingham Festival in England. William Bartholomew was given the *Elijah* libretto in the middle of May, 1846, and was engaged to translate it into English for the August premiere, receiving sections as they were completed. Mendelssohn and Schubring had used Luther's translation of the Bible, interpolating and paraphrasing liberally. Bartholomew's task was not only to translate, but also to make the text agree with the King James Bible. He added the following disclaimer to the libretto of *Elijah:* "The author of this English version has endeavored to render it as nearly in accordance with the Scriptural Texts as the Music to which it is adapted will admit: the references are therefore to be considered rather as authorities than quotations."

The arias are presented in both English, the language of the premiere, and German, the working language of Mendelssohn's composition. It was clearly the composer's intention that English speaking audiences hear the piece in the vernacular.

Lord God of Abraham (Herr Gott Abrahams)

From Part I. Just after the chorus has dramatically called to Baal, the pagan god, to hear and answer, Elijah interrupts the silence with this prayer to the Lord God of Abraham, Isaac, and Israel.

Is not his word like a fire? (Ist nicht des Herrn Wort wie ein Feuer?)

From Part I. Elijah's fiery sermon about God's righteous anger against allegiance to pagan gods, coming just after the chorus sings "Take all the prophets of Baal, and let not one of them escape us, bring all, and slay them!"

It is enough! (Es ist genug!)

From Part II. Elijah has been threatened with revenge by Jezebel, and to save himself has taken refuge in the wilderness, where he laments his cowardice.

For the mountains shall depart (Ja, es sollen wohl Berge weichen)

From Part II. Elijah's final words of peace before being taken up to heaven in a whirlwind of fire.

PAULUS
(St. Paul)
1836
libretto by J. Schubring, after the Acts of the Apostles

Composition began in 1834. The oratorio was originally commissioned for the St. Cecilia Society in Frankfurt, but because of the presenter's illness, the premiere was instead given at the Düsseldorf Festival (for which Mendelssohn was a director) on May 22, 1836. The piece was heavily revised for the first published edition (1837, Novello), which contained German and English. The revised *Paulus* was performed in March of 1837 in Frankfurt.

Gott sei mir gnädig

Gott sei mir gnädig
nach deiner Güte,
und tilge meine Sünden
nach deiner grossen Barmherzigkeit.
Verwirf mich nicht
von deinem Angesicht und nimm
deinen heiligen Geist
nicht von mir.
Ein geängstetes und
zerschlagenes Herz
wirst du Gott nicht verachten.
Denn ich will die Uebertreter
deine Wege lehren,
dass sich die Sünder
zu dir bekehren.
Herr thue meine Lippen auf,
dass mein Mund deinem Ruhm verkündige.
Herr! verwirf mich nicht!

[O God, have mercy]

God to me be merciful
according to you goodness,
and blot out my sins
according to your great mercy.
Spurn me not
from your face and take
your Holy Spirit
not from me.
A contrite and
broken heart
will you God not despise.
Then I will the tresspasser
your ways teach,
that the sinner
to you convert.
Lord open my lips,
that my mouth your glory make known.
Lord! cast me not away!

Giacomo Puccini

1858-1924

MESSA DI GLORIA

1880
text is the traditional Latin Mass from the Roman Catholic liturgy

Composed in 1880 as Puccini's final exam at the conservatory at Lucca. The mass also contains a Mottetto and a Credo that date from 1878. First performed July 12, 1880, Lucca, on the feast-day of St. Paulino (the patron saint of bells).

Crucifixus

Crucifixus etiam pro nobis
passus et sepultus est,
crucifixus etiam pro nobis
sub Pontio Pilato.

Crucified also for us
suffered and was buried,
crucified also for us
under Pontias Pilate.

Gioachino Rossini

1792-1868

MESSE SOLENNELLE

1864
text is the traditional Latin Mass from the Roman Catholic liturgy

Composed in 1863, first performed in Paris, March 14, 1864, for the dedication of the private chapel of Countess Louise Pillet-Will. This original version was for 4 soloists, a chorus of 8 voices, 2 pianos and harmonium. The piece is often called "Petite Messe Solennelle," referring to the chamber music scale of the design, not because of brevity or liturgical reasons. Revised in 1867 for full orchestra; revision performed in Paris, February 24, 1869.

Quoniam tu solus sanctus

Quoniam tu solus sanctus, Tu solus Dominus,
Tu solus altisimus Jesu Christe.

For you alone are holy, You alone are Lord,
You alone are most high Jesus Christ.

STABAT MATER

1832; 1842
text is traditional Latin from the Roman Catholic liturgy, a 13th century sequence attributed to the Franciscon Jacopone da Todi

First performed on Good Friday, 1833 at Cappella di San Filippo El Real, Madrid. Due to illness, Rossini requested that Giovanni Tadolini compose six of the twelve sections in order to complete the work for the premiere. In 1841 Rossini replaced the six Tadolini movements with new composition. The revised Stabat Mater was first performed January 7, 1842 at the Théâtre Italien, Paris. Stabat Mater (literally translated as "mother standing") refers to Mary standing at the base of the cross.

Pro peccatis

Pro peccatis suæ gentis vidit Jesum in tormentis,
et flagellis subditum.
Vidit suum dulcem natum morientem desolatum
dum emisit spiritum.

In place of mankind she saw Jesus in torment
and scourged in the their place.
Saw her sweet child dying forsaken
until he sent forth his spirit.

Giuseppe Verdi

1813-1901

MESSA DI REQUIEM

1874
text is the traditional Latin Requiem Mass from the Roman Catholic liturgy; Requiem ("rest") is a Mass for the dead

The piece has a long history of development. In November, 1868, Verdi sent his publisher, Ricordi, a letter proposing a Requiem Mass, written by Italian composers, to honor Rossini, who had died early in the month. There was to be one performance only, on the first anniversary of Rossini's death, and no one was to profit from the work. Verdi was assigned the "Libera me" section of the mass, and completed composition in August. Severe conflicts and controversies prevented the "Rossini Requiem" from being presented. (It wasn't heard until 1988 at the Parma Cathedral.) In 1873 the Italian novelist Alessandro Manzoni died. Verdi proposed to Ricordi that he would write a Requiem in honor of Manzoni, and like the "Rossini Requiem," wanted to have the first performance on the first anniversary of Manzoni's death. Verdi incorporated the "Libera me" section that he had composed five years earlier. The Messa di Requiem was first performed May 22, 1874 at the Church of San Marco, Milan.

Confutatis

Confutatis maledictis,
Flammis acribus addictis,
Voca me cum benedictis.
Oro supplex et acclinis,
Cor contritum quasi cinis,
Gere curam mei finis.

Repressed, confused,
Judged to pass through flames,
Call me with the blessed.
Humbly pleading on my knees,
My heart's contrition, like ashes,
Bears the anxiety of my end.

The Arias

Fecit potentiam
from
MAGNIFICAT

Carl Philipp Emanuel Bach

17
21
25
[mf]
Fe - cit po - ten - ti - am, fe - cit po -
29
ten - ti - am, fe - cit po - ten - ti - am in bra - chio
tr
f
p

su - o, po - ten - ti - am, po - ten - ti - am in bra - chio
su - o: dis - per - sit su - per - bos, su -
per - bos dis - per - sit, dis - per - sit su - per - bos men - te
cor - dis su - i. Dis -

49
per - sit,
dis - per - sit
su -
f
mf
p
f
mf
p
p
53
per - bos,
dis - per
57
- sit su - per - bos
men - te
cor - dis
su -
tr
61
i,
dis - per - sit
su - per - bos,
su - per - bos
men - te
f
p
tr
tr
tr

65
tr
cor - dis su - i.
f
69
73
tr
tr
tr
77
Fe - cit po -
p

81
ten - ti - am, fe - cit po - ten - ti - am, fe - cit po -
85
ten - ti - am in bra - chio su - o, po - ten - ti - am
89
fe - cit in bra - chio su - o, po - ten - ti - am
93
fe - cit in bra - chio su - o, po - ten -

97

\- - - - - - -

101

\- - ti-am fe-cit, po - ten - ti - am, po -

105

ten - ti - am in bra - chio su - o. Dis -

109

per - sit su - per - bos, su - per - bos dis - per - sit, dis -

113
per - - - - - - sit su-
117
per-bos men-te cor - dis su - i.
tr
f
122
Dis - per-sit, dis - per-sit su-
p
f
p
f
f
p
127
per - bos, dis - per - - - -

131

- sit su - per - bos __ men - te cor - dis __ su -

tr

135

i, dis - per - sit su - per - bos, su - per - bos men - te

f tr tr tr

139

tr tr

cor - dis __ su - i.

f tr tr

143

tr

Quia fecit mihi magna
from
MAGNIFICAT

Johann Sebastian Bach

10

po - - - - - tens, qui po - tens

13

est; qui - a fe - cit mi - hi ma -

18
e - jus, et sanc - tum no - men, et sanc-tum no-men
20
e - jus, sanc - tum no-men e - jus, sanc-tum no - men e - jus, et
tr
23
sanc - tum no - men e - jus;

25

qui - a fe - cit mi - hi ma - gna, qui po - tens _

27

est, et sanc - - tum no - men, sanc - tum _

29

no - men _ e - jus.

32

Et in Spiritum sanctum
from
MASS IN B MINOR

Johann Sebastian Bach

21
tr
tr
25
et in Spi - ri - tum sanc - tum Do - mi - num et vi - vi - fi - can -
p
29
tem, vi - vi - fi - can - tem, Spi - ri - tum sanc - tum, Spi - ri - tum
33
sanc - tum vi - vi - fi - can - tem, vi - vi - fi - can - tem Do - mi - num, qui ex

37
Pa - tre Fi - li - o - que pro - ce -
41
- - - dit, ex Pa - tre Fi - li - o - que pro -
45
ce - dit, qui ex Pa - tre Fi - li - o - que pro - ce - dit;
tr
tr
50

55
60
qui _ cum Pa - tre et Fi - li - o si-mul a - do-
p
65
ra - tur, a - do - ra - - - - -
69
- tur et con - glo - ri - fi - ca - -

73
tur, et con - glo - ri - fi - ca - tur;
77
qui lo - cu-tus est per Pro - phe - tas, lo -
82
cu - tus est per Pro - phe - tas, per Pro - phe-tas lo - cu - tus est,
86
lo - cu - tus est per Pro - phe - tas, lo - cu - tus est per Pro -

phe - tas, per Pro - phe - tas.
Et un-am sanc-tam ca-tho-li-cam
et a-po-sto - li - cam_ ec-cle - si-am,
tr
tr
et u-nam sanc-tam ca-tho-li-cam et a-po-sto - li - cam_ ec-cle - si -
p

109
am, et u-nam sanc - tam ca-tho - -
113
- - - - - li-cam_ et a-po-
117
sto-li-cam_ec-cle - - - si-am, u-
122
- nam_ sanc - tam ca-tho-li-cam et a-po-sto-li-cam_ ec-cle -

126
- si - am, u - nam sanc - tam ca - tho - li - cam et a - po - sto -
130
- li - cam_ ec - cle - si - am.
135
140
tr
tr

Betrachte, meine Seel'
(Consider, O my soul)
from
PASSIO SECUNDUM JOANNEM
(St. John Passion)

Johann Sebastian Bach

*appoggiatura possible

6

höch - stes Gut in Je - su Schmer - zen, wie dir ___ auf
high - est staff is Je - sus' an - guish. For you ___ the

8

Dor - nen, so ihn ste - chen, die Him-mels-schlüs-sel-blu - men blüh'n, du
thorn - crown that did pierce Him, With heav - en - scent - ed flow'rs _ will bloom; You

10

kannst viel süs - se Frucht von sei - ner Wer - mut bre - chen, drum
can the sweet - est fruit a - mong His worm - wood gath - er then

12
sieh ohn' Un - ter - lass auf Ihn, auf Ihn, drum sieh ohn'
look to raise your eyes to Him, to Him, then look to
14
Un - ter - lass auf Ihn, ohn' Un - ter - lass, drum sieh ohn' Un - ter - lass auf
raise your eyes to Him, cease not to raise your eyes, to raise your eyes to
16
Ihn.
Him.

Gerne will ich mich bequemen

(Gladly would I be enduring)

from

PASSIO SECUNDUM MATTHÆUM

(St. Matthew Passion)

Johann Sebastian Bach

Recit.
[Andante]
Der Hei-land fällt vor sein-em Vat - er nie - der, da - durch er-hebt er mich und
The Sav - ior, low be-fore His Fa - ther ben - ding, Would bring to pass, by His ob -
[p]
simile
3
al - le von un - serm Fal - le hi - nauf zu Got - tes Gna - de wie - der.
la - tion, A full sal - va - tion, The love of God to man com-mend - ing.
5
Er ist be - reit, den Kelch, des To - des Bit - ter - keit zu
Pre - pared is He, the cup, al - tho' it bit - ter be, To

7
trin - ken, in welch-en Sün - den die - ser Welt ge - gos - sen sind und häss - lich
drink, The which with sins of men is filled, And o - ver - flows. He would not
9
stin - ken, weil es dem lie - ben Gott ge - fällt.
shrink, But suf - fer all that God hath willed.
Aria
[f]
7
tr

13
Ger - ne will ich mich be - que - men Kreuz und Be - cher
Glad - ly would I be en - dur - ing Grief and pain, if
p
19
an - zu - neh - men, trink ich doch dem Hei - land nach,
so se - cur - ing That I fol - low Christ, my Lord,
25
ger - ne will ich
Glad - ly would I
p

31
mich be - que - men,
be en - dur - ing,
ger - ne,
glad - ly,
ger - ne,
glad - ly,
37
ger - ne will ich mich be - que - men
glad - ly would I be en - dur - ing
Kreuz und Be - cher
Grief and pain, if
43
an - zu - neh - men, trink ich doch dem Hei - land nach, trink
so se - cur - ing That I fol - low Christ, my Lord, that
tr

49
ich doch dem Hei - land nach, Kreuz und Be - cher an -
I fol - low Christ, my Lord, Glad - ly would I be
55
- zu - neh - men, will ich ger - ne mich be - que - men,
en - dur - ing Grief and pain, if so se - cur - ing
61
trink ich doch dem Hei - land nach.
That I fol - low Christ, my Lord.
f

67
tr
*
Fine

72
Denn sein Mund, der mit Milch und Ho - nig flies - set,
Lo, His love, All our sor - rows free - ly shar - ing,
p

78
hat den Grund und des Lei - dens her - be Schmach durch den er -
Doth re - move Half its weight from shame ab - horred, Now that He

*Fermata on Fine

Da Capo al Fine

Komm, süsses Kreuz
(Come, healing cross)
from
PASSIO SECUNDUM MATTHÆUM
(St. Matthew Passion)

Johann Sebastian Bach

Aria

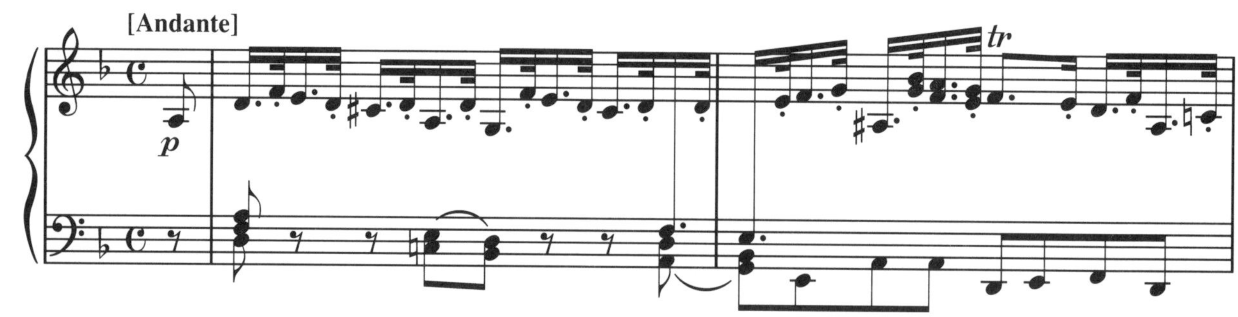
[Andante]
p
tr

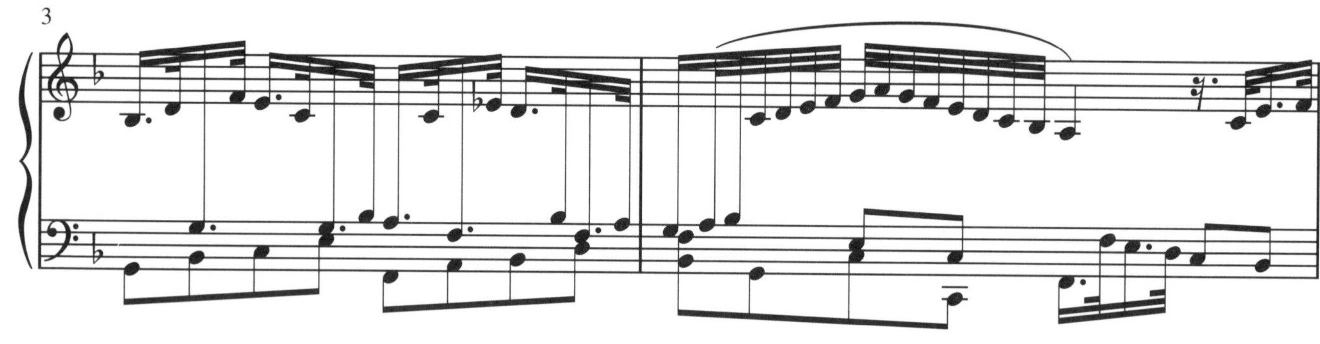
3

5
f

7
Komm,
Come,

9
süs - ses Kreuz, komm, süs - ses Kreuz, komm,
heal - ing Cross, come, heal - ing Cross, come,
tr
11
süs - ses Kreuz, so will ich
heal - ing Cross, for me pre -
12
sa - gen, mein Je - su,
pare it, My Sav - ior,
13
gib es im - mer her, komm, süs - ses Kreuz, komm,
lay on me its weight, Come, heal - ing Cross, come,

15

süs - ses _ Kreuz, so will ich ___ sa - gen, mein Je - su, _ gib es im - mer _

heal - ing _ Cross, for me pre - pare _ it, My Sav - ior, _ lay on me _ its _

cresc.

17

her, komm, süs - ses ___ Kreuz, ________________ so will ich

weight, Come, heal - ing ___ Cross, ________________ for me pre -

18

sa - gen, mein Je - su, gib es im - mer her!

pare ___ it, My Sav - ior, lay on me its weight;

20

tr

22
tr
Wird mir _ mein _
When-e'er _ my ___
24
Lei - - - - - - -
bur - - - - - - -
25
- den einst zu schwer, zu schwer, _ zu schwer, mein _ Lei -
- den grows too great, too great, _ too great, _ my _ bur -
27
- - - - - den einst zu
- - - - - den grows too

28
schwer, zu schwer, zu schwer, so hilf du mir
great, too great, too great, To Thee I look
cresc.
30
es sel - ber tra - - -
for help to bear
31
32
gen, so hilf du mir es sel - ber
it, to Thee I look for help to

33
tra - gen, so hilf du mir es sel-ber tra - gen.
bear it, to Thee I look for help to bear it.
35
37
39
Komm, süs - ses Kreuz, komm,
Come, heal - ing Cross, come,

41
süs - ses Kreuz, komm, süs - ses Kreuz, so will ich
heal - ing Cross, come, heal - ing Cross, for me pre -
tr
43
sa - gen, mein Je - su,
pare it, My Sav - ior,
44
gib es im - mer her, komm, süs - ses Kreuz, komm,
lay on me its weight, Come, heal - ing Cross, come,
46
süs - ses Kreuz, so will ich sa - gen, mein Je - su, gib es im - mer
heal - ing Cross, for me pre - pare it, My Sav - ior, lay on me its

48
her, komm, süs - ses Kreuz, so will ich
weight, Come, heal - ing Cross, for me pre -
49
sa - gen, mein Je - su, gib es im - mer her!
pare it, My Sav - ior, lay on me its weight.
51
a tempo
tr
53

Mache dich, mein Herze, rein

(Make thee clean, my heart)
from
PASSIO SECUNDUM MATTHÆUM
(St. Matthew Passion)

Johann Sebastian Bach

7
Mun - de. O schö - ne Zeit! O A - bend -
bore. O beau - teous time, O eve - ning
9
stun - de! Der Frie - dens - schluss ist nun mit Gott ge -
hour! Our peace with God is ev - er - more as -
11
macht, denn Je - sus hat sein Kreuz voll - bracht. Sein
sured, For Je - sus hath His Cross en - dured. His

13

Leich - nam kommt zur Ruh. Ach, lie - be See - le, bit - te

bod - y thou dost crave, Thou, His dis - ci - ple, for the

15

du, geh, las - se dir den to - ten Je - sum schen - ken, o

grave. O let us all re - gard with thank - ful won - der His

17

heil - sa - mes, o köst - lich's An - ge - den - ken!

pre - cious death, and on its mean - ing pon - der.

Aria

[Andante]
[p]

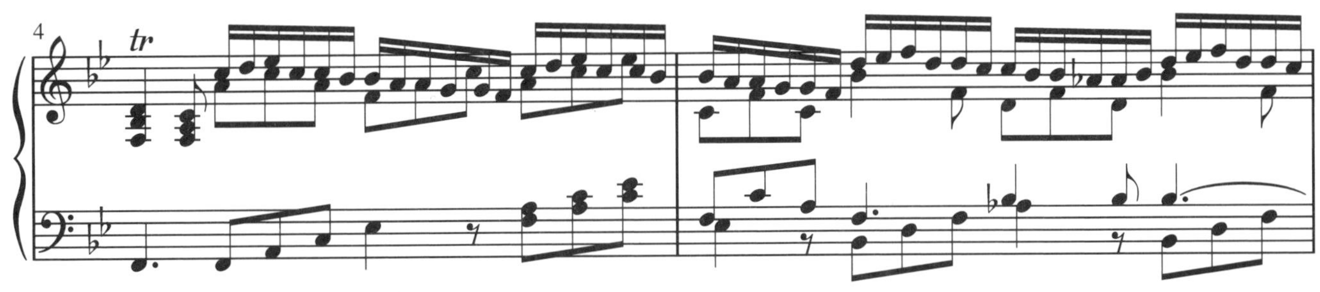
4
tr

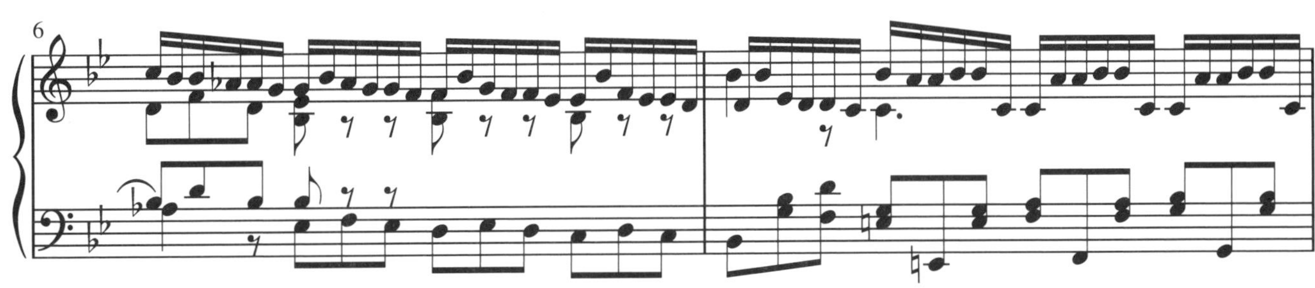
6

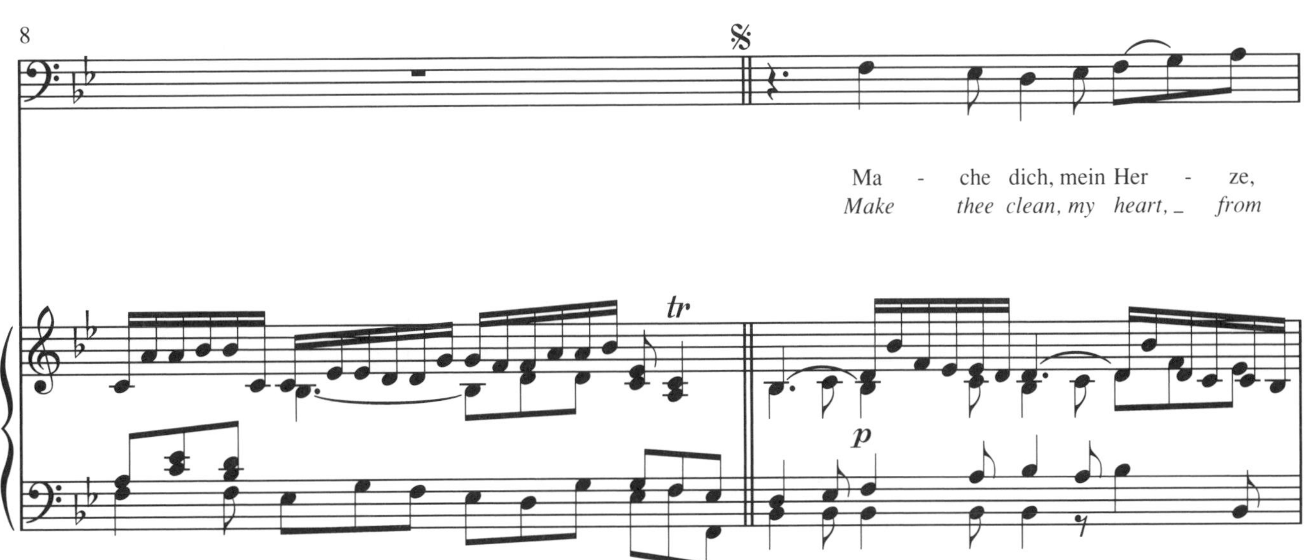
8
Ma - che dich, mein Her - ze,
Make thee clean, my heart, from
tr
p

10
rein, ___
sin, ___
ma - che dich, mein Her - ze,
make thee clean, my heart, _ from
13
rein, ___ ich will Je - sum _ selbst be - gra - ben, _ ich will Je - sum _ selbst be - gra-ben,
sin, ___ Un-to Je - sus _ wel-come giv - ing, _ un-to Je - sus _ wel-come giv-ing,
tr
tr
f
16
ma - che dich, mein Her - ze, rein,
Make _ thee clean, my heart, _ from sin,
f

18
ma - che dich, mein Her - ze, rein, ich will Je - sum selbst be -
make thee clean, my heart, from sin, un-to Je - sus wel-come
mf
20
gra - ben, ich will Je - sum selbst be - gra - - -
giv - ing, un-to Je - sus wel-come giv - - -
tr
22
- - - ben, ma - che dich, mein Her - ze,
- - - ing, make thee clean, my heart, from

24

rein, ich will Je - sum selbst ______ be - gra - - - -
sin, un - to Je - sus wel - come giv - - - -

26

ben, ______ ma - che dich, _ mein Her - ze, rein, ich ______ will Je - sum selbst ______ be -
ing, ______ make thee clean, _ my heart, _ from sin, un - to Je - sus wel - come

28

gra - ben, ich will Je - sum selbst _ be - gra - ben,
giv - ing, un - to Je - sus wel - come giv - ing.

tr

f

f

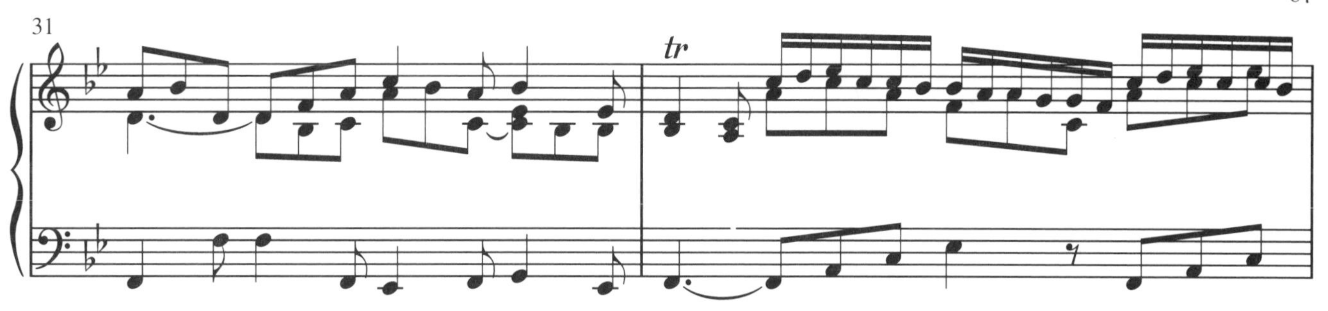

*Fermata on Fine

39
_ für und für sei-ne süs - se Ru - he ha - ben, denn er ___ soll nun -
_ shall He rest, Ev - er - more _ with-in ___ me liv - ing, So with - in my
41
mehr __ in mir für ___ und für ___ sei-ne süs - se Ru -
cleans - ed breast Shall ___ He rest, ___ Ev - er - more _ with - in ___
43
- - - he ha - ben, sei - ne süs-se _ Ru - he ha -
me liv - ing, ev - er - more with-in _ me liv -

Dal Segno al Fine

Grosser Herr und starker König

(Mighty Lord and King all glorious)
from
WEIHNACHTS-ORATORIUM
(Christmas Oratorio)

Johann Sebastian Bach

17
star - ker Kö - nig, lieb - ster Hei - land o wie
King all - glo - rious, Sav - ior true, for man vic -
22
we - nig ach - test du der Er - den Pracht, der Er - den
to - rious, Earth - ly state Thou dost dis - dain, Thou dost dis -
28
Pracht! Gros - ser Herr und star - ker Kö - nig,
dain. Might - y Lord and King all - glo - rious,
tr

33
tr
lieb - ster Hei - land, o wie we - nig ach -
Sav - ior true, for man vic - to - rious, Earth -
38
- test du der Er - den Pracht, lieb - ster Hei - land,
- ly state Thou dost dis - dain. Might - y Lord,
43
gros - ser Herr und star - ker Kö - nig, o wie we - nig
might - y Lord and King all - glo - rious, Earth-ly state Thou

48
ach - test du der Er - den Pracht! Gros - ser Herr und
dost dis - dain, Thou dost dis - dain. Might - y Lord, and
tr
53
star - ker Kö - nig, lieb - ster Hei - land, o wie we -
King all glo - rious, Sav - ior true, for man vic - to -
tr
58
- nig ach - test du der Er - den Pracht,
- rious, Earth - ly state Thou dost dis - dain,

*Fermata on Fine

84
hält, die gan-ze Welt, die gan - ze Welt er - hält,
tain, who all things, who all things doth sus - tain,
89
ih - re Pracht und Zier er - schaf-fen, muss in har -
Who all state and pomp sup - pli - eth, In a low -
94
- ten Krip-pen schla - fen.
- ly man-ger li - eth.
tr
f

100
tr
105
Der die ganze, die ganze Welt erhält,
He who all things, who all things doth sustain,
p
110
die ganze Welt erhält, ihre Pracht
who all things doth sustain, Who all state
115
und Zier erschaffen, muss in harten Krippen schlafen.
and pomp supplieth, In a lowly manger lieth.
tr
Da Capo al Fine

O misère des rois!
from
L'ENFANCE DU CHRIST

Hector Berlioz

Recit.
HÉRODES: sotto voce
13
Tou-jours ce rê - ve!
f
p
17
f
en - co - re cet en - fant . . .
Qui doit me dé - trô -
f
20
ner!
Et ne sa - voir que cro - e
p
pp
23
De ce pré - sa - ge me-na - çant
Pour ma vie et ma gloi - re! . . .
pp
ff

26
Andante misterioso (♩ = 60)
ff
ff
mf
p simile
30
34
sf
p
f
38
O mi - sè - re des rois! Ré - gner et ne pas
p
dim.
poco f
p

43

vi - vre! A tous don - ner — des lois,

poco ***f*** ***p*** *dim.*

48

poco ***f***

Et dé - si - rer de sui - vre Le che - vri -

poco ***f*** ***p***

poco ***f*** ***p***

52

er, le che - vri - er au fond des bois! —

rinf. ***p***

56
p
O nuit pro - fon - de Qui tiens le mon - de Dans le re - pos plon -
p
p
perdendo
cresc.

61
gé, A mon sein ra - va - gé Don - ne la

65
paix une heu - re, Et que ton voi - le ef - fleu - re Mon
espr.

69
front d'en - nuis char - gé! . . .
sf
mf
dim.
73
A mon sein ra - va - gé
pp
p
77
Don - ne la paix une heu - re!
81
O mi - sè - re des rois!
sf
pp

85
O mi - sè - re des rois! Ré -
89
gner et ne pas vi - vre! A tous don-ner des lois, Et
93
dé-si-rer de sui-vre Le che-vri-er, le che-vri-er au fond des

97
bois!
f
f
dim.
f

101
p
Ef-fort sté - ri - le! Le som-meil fuit;
p
sempre smorz.

105
Un poco rit.
Et ma plainte i - nu - ti - le Ne hâ - te point ton cours,
Un poco rit.
ppp

109
sf
Un poco rit.
a tempo
vibrato
in - ter - mi - na - ble nuit, in - ter - mi - na - ble
Un poco rit.
poco sf
poco sf
a tempo
poco sf
p
113
nuit!
pp
p
p
117
121
a tempo
sf
sf
(p)
cresc. molto
f
p
pp

Hostias
from
REQUIEM

Gabriel Fauré

12
cresc.
fe - ri - mus ta sus - ci - pe
mf

15
dim. *p* *dolce*
pro a - ni - ma - bus il - lis qua - rum
dim.
p

18
ho - di - e me - mo - ri - am

21
mf
— fa - ci - mus,
mf
pp
24
p
28
p
p
fac e - as, fac e - as Do - mi - ne de mor - te tran -
32
pp
si - re ad vi - tam

35
meno p
quam o - lim A - bra - hae pro - mi -
espress.
39
dim.
sis - ti, pro - mi - sis - ti et
f
pp
44
mf
p
se - mi - ni e - jus.
f
p

Revenge, Timotheus cries
from
ALEXANDER'S FEAST

George Frideric Handel

14
re - venge, Tim - o-theus cries.
17
See, the fu - ries a - rise! See, the
20
snakes that they rear, how they hiss in the air! and the
22
spar - kles that flash in their eyes, and the

24
spar - - - - - kles, the spar-kles that
27
flash in their eyes! Re - venge, Tim - o-theus cries, re - venge, Tim - o-theus cries, re -
30
venge, re-venge, re - venge, re-venge! See, the
33
fu - ries a-rise! See, the snakes that they rear, how they hiss _ in the air!

36
and the spar - - - -
p
39
- - - kles that flash,
42
and the spark - les that flash in their eyes!
f
46
Fine

Largo
Be - hold a ghast-ly
band, a ghast - ly band, each a torch in his hand, each a
[p]
[f]
tr

torch in his hand! These are Grec - ian ghosts, that in bat - tle were slain, and un-
[p]
bur - ied re - main, in - glor - ious on the _ plain, in - glor - ious
[f]
on ___ the plain! There are Gre - cian ghosts, that in bat - tle were slain, and un -
p
bur - ied re - main, in - glo - rious on the plain,
[f]
p
f

Da Capo al Fine

See the raging flames arise
from
JOSHUA

Recit.

George Frideric Handel

*The final 2 chords are usually played following the finish of the vocal line.

Aria

13
see the ra-ging flames a -
f
p
16
rise, the rag - ing flames
19
a - rise;
Hear,
22
hear the dis - mal groans and cries, the dis - mal groans and
p

25
cries, hear the dis - mal groans, the dis - mal groans and
29
cries:
f
33
The fa - tal_ day of wrath is come, Proud
p
36
Je - ri-cho hath met her_ doom, The fa - tal day is come, the fa - tal day of

39
wrath, the fa - tal day of wrath is come, Proud
42
Je - ri - cho hath met her doom, proud Je - ri-cho hath met her
45
doom,
f
48
Hear the dis - mal groans and cries, hear the dis-mal
p

52
groans, hear, hear the dis - mal cries, See, see the rag - ing flames a -
56
rise, the ra - ging flames
59
a - rise, The fa - tal day,
62
the day of wrath is come, the day of wrath is

66

come, Proud Je - ri-cho hath met her doom, proud ___

69 **Adagio** **a tempo**

Je - ri-cho hath met her doom, proud Je - ri-cho hath met her doom.

f

73

77

Behold the monstrous human beast

from

BELSHAZZAR

George Frideric Handel

16
ces-sive feast, Wal - lowing, wal - lowing; wal -
p
20
- - - - low-ing in ex - ces - sive feast.
f
23
Be - hold the mon - strous
p
26
hu - man beast, the mon - strous beast, Be - hold the mon-strous beast, the

29
mon - strous _ hu - man beast,
Wal - lowing,
wal - lowing,
f
32
wal - - - - lowing, wal - lowing in ___ ex -
p
35
ces - sive feast,
Wal - lowing in ex - ces - sive feast.
f
39
No more his mak - er's im - age found,
But, self - de - grad - ed
p
Fine

43
to a swine, He fix - es, grov - 'ling, on the ground, He
46
fix - es, grov - 'ling, grov - 'ling grov - 'ling,
f
p
49
on the ground His por - tion of the breath Di-vine, His
52
por - tion of the breath Di-vine. Be-
f
Dal Segno al Fine

Arm, arm, ye brave!
from
JUDAS MACCABÆUS

George Frideric Handel

Recit.
[Maestoso]
SIMON:
I feel,
[f]
4
I feel the De - i - ty with - in,
Who, the bright
7
Cher - u - bim be - tween,
His ra - diant glo - ry erst dis - play'd;
To

10
Is - ra - el's dis - tress - ful pray'r he hath vouch - saf'd a gra - cious

12
ear, And points out Mac - ca - bæ - us to their aid: Ju - das shall set the cap - tive

15
free, And lead us on to vic - to - ry.

Aria

Allegro
f
5
Arm, arm, ye brave! Arm, arm, ye brave! a
p
10
no - ble cause, a no - ble cause, The cause of Heav'n, your
f
p
14
zeal de-mands, a no - ble cause, the cause of Heav'n, your zeal de-mands, a

18
no - ble cause, the cause of Heav'n, your zeal de - mands.
22
Arm, arm, ye brave! arm, arm, ye brave! a
26
no - ble cause! Arm, arm, arm, arm, ye brave! Arm, arm,
31
arm, arm, ye brave! A no - ble cause, the cause of Heav'n, your zeal de-mands, your

35
zeal ___ de-mands; Arm, arm, ye brave! A no - ble cause, the cause of Heav'n, your
f
p
39
zeal de-mands, your zeal, the cause of Heav'n your zeal de -
f
p
f
44
mands!
48
In de - fence of your na - tion, re - li - gion and laws, The al -
p

52
might - y Je - ho - vah will streng-then your hands;
In de - fence of your na - tion,
56
re - li - gion and laws,
The al-might - y Je - ho - vah will
60
strength - - - - - en, the al -
64
might - y Je - hov - ah will sreng - then your hands.

68
Arm, arm, arm, arm, ye brave! a
71
no - ble cause, The cause of Heav'n, your zeal de-mands, a no - ble cause,
75
arm, arm, ye brave! Arm, arm, ye brave! The cause of Heav'n, your zeal de -
79
mands!

Thus saith the Lord; But who may abide

from

MESSIAH

George Frideric Handel

12
— and I will shake
all na-tions; I'll
p
15
shake the heav'ns, the earth, the sea, the
17
dry land, all na - tions, I'll shake, and the de -
19
sire

21
(Recit.)
of all na - tions shall come.
The Lord whom ye
f
24
seek shall sud-den-ly come to His tem - ple,
ev'n the mes-sen-ger of the cov - e-nant,
27
whom ye de-light in;
Be-hold, he shall come,
saith the Lord of Hosts.
Aria
Andante larghetto
f

6
13
But who may a - bide the day of His com - ing, the
21
day of His com - ing, but who may a - bide the day of His com - ing,
28
the day of His com - ing, and who shall

35
stand when He ap - pear - eth, when He ap - pear - eth?
[f]
41
when He ap - pear - eth? and who shall stand when He ap -
[p]
p
47
pear - eth?
But who may a - bide, but
[f]
[p]
53
who may a - bide the day of His com - ing,
but who may a -
[f]
[p]

60
bide the day of His com - ing, and who shall
67
stand when He ap - pear-eth? and who shall stand when He ap -
75
pear - eth?
f
82
For He is like a re - fi - ner's fire,
p

89
95
for He is
100
like a re - fi - ner's fire,
106

112
Adagio
for He is like a re - fi -
118
Tempo I
- ner's fire.
f
124
131

For behold, darkness shall cover the earth; The people that walked in darkness

from

MESSIAH

George Frideric Handel

9
peo - ple,
and gross dark - ness the peo - ple:
11
but the Lord shall a - rise
13
up - on thee, and His
15
glo - - ry shall be seen up - on thee, and His

18
glo - ry shall be seen up - on thee. And the Gen-tiles shall
21
f
come to thy light, and kings to the bright - ness of thy ris - ing.
Aria
Larghetto
f
4
The peo - ple that walk - ed in dark - ness, that
p

*Both notes are in Handel's manuscript.

16
walk - ed in dark - ness have seen a great light,
19
p
the peo - ple that walk - ed, that walk - ed in dark - ness, that
22
walk - ed in dark - ness, the peo - ple that walk - ed in dark -

26
- ness have seen a great light, have seen a great light,
29
a great light, have seen a great light:
32
and

35
they _ that _ dwell, ___ that dwell _ in the land _ of the shad -
38
- ow of death, ________ and
41
they _ that _ dwell, _ that _ dwell _ in the land, ___ that dwell _ in the land _ of the

44
shad - ow of death, up -
47
on them hath the light shin - ed, and
f
p
50
they that dwell, that dwell in the land of the shad -

53
- ow of death, up - on them hath the

56
light shin - ed, up - on them hath the light shin - ed.
f

60

Why do the nations
from
MESSIAH

George Frideric Handel

11
13
15
Why do the na - tions so
p
17
fu - rious - ly rage to - geth - er? why

19
do the peo - ple im - a - gine a vain
21
thing? Why do the na - tions
23
3
rage
25
so
[f]
[p]

27
fu - rious - ly ___ to - geth - er?
why
f
p
30
do the peo - ple im - a - - -
3
32
- - - - gine ___ a ___ vain ___
34
thing? ___ im - a - -

36
- gine _ a vain thing?
f
39
Why do the na - tions so fu - rious - ly rage __ to -
p
42
geth - er, and why do the
[f]
[p]
44
peo - ple, and why do the

46
peo - ple
im
-
a
-
gine
a
vain
48
thing?
Why
do
the
na
-
tions
50
3
rage
52

54
— so fu - rious - ly to - geth-er, so fu - rious - ly to - geth - er? and
57
why do the peo - ple im - a - gine a vain
60
thing? im - a - - -
f
62
- gine a vain thing? and

64
why do the peo - ple im - a - gine a vain
68
thing?
f
71
74
The kings of the earth rise up, and the
p

77
rul - ers take coun - sel to - geth - er, take
79
3
coun - - - - - - -
81
- - - - sel, take
83
coun - sel to - geth - er a-gainst the Lord, and a -

86
gainst His an - oint - - - -
3
89
3
- - - - - - - -
91
- ed, a - gainst the Lord and His an -
93
oint - - - - - - ed.

The trumpet shall sound
from
MESSIAH

George Frideric Handel

*Small size notes are to be played only in the absence of a trumpet.

12
17
22
[tr]
p
28
The trum-pet shall sound, and the dead shall be
p
34
raised, and the dead shall be raised in-cor-

40
rup - ti - ble;
the
f
45
trum - pet shall sound,
and the dead shall be
p
p
50
raised,
be rasied in - cor - rup - ti - ble,
be
55
raised in - cor - rup - ti - ble,
and we shall be chang'd,
f
p

61
66
— and we shall be chang'd.
f
72
tr
77
The trum - pet shall sound, the
p

83
trum - pet shall sound,
and the dead shall be raised,
89
be raised in - cor - rup - ti - ble,
94
be raised in - cor - rup - ti - ble,
and
100
we shall be chang'd, be chang'd,

105
and we shall be chang'd,
110
and we shall be chang'd,
we
115
shall be chang'd,
we shall be
120
chang'd,
and we shall be chang'd,

125

and we shall be

130

chang'd, we shall be chang'd, ___

135

and we shall be chang'd, we shall be chang'd.

Adagio

Tempo I

f

141

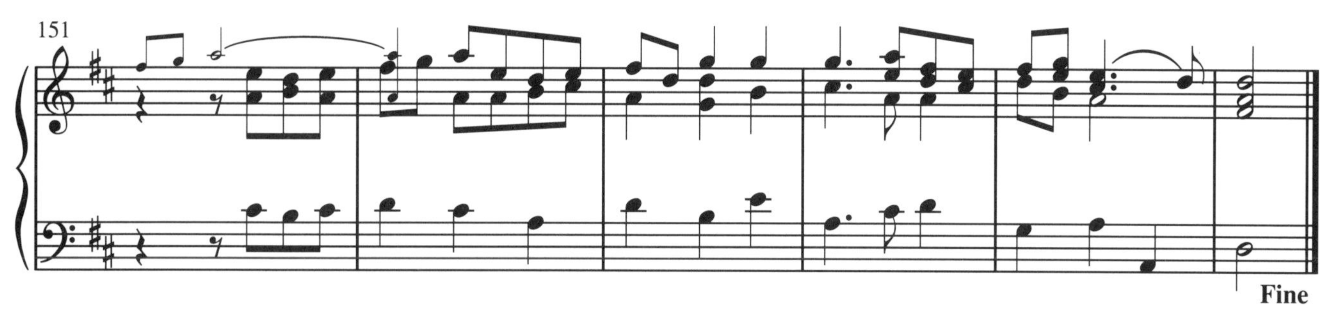

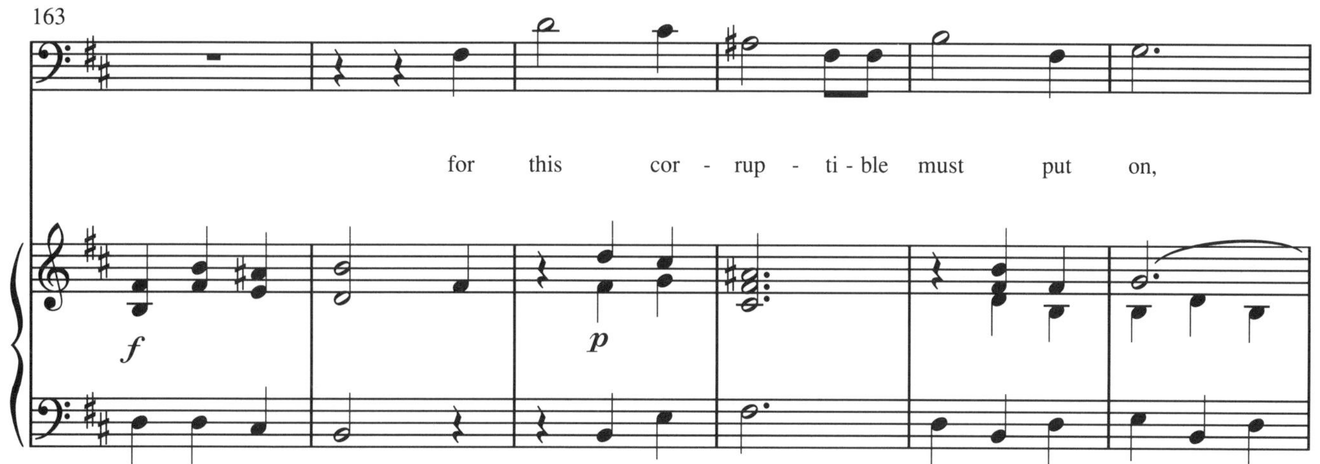

*This section and the *da capo* are often cut in performances of *Messiah*.

169
must put on,
174
must put on, must put on in - cor - rup - tion;
f
180
and this mor - tal must put on im - mor -
p
186
tal - - - - - -

191
- - - - - i - ty, and this
196
mor - tal must _ put on im - mor - tal -
202
- - - - - - -
208
- i - ty, im - mor - tal - i - ty.
3
Dal Segno al Fine

The trumpet shall sound
from
MESSIAH

George Frideric Handel

The part may be carefully cut from the book.

Tacet on "B" section (57 measures).

Thy glorious deeds inspir'd my tongue

from

SAMSON

George Frideric Handel

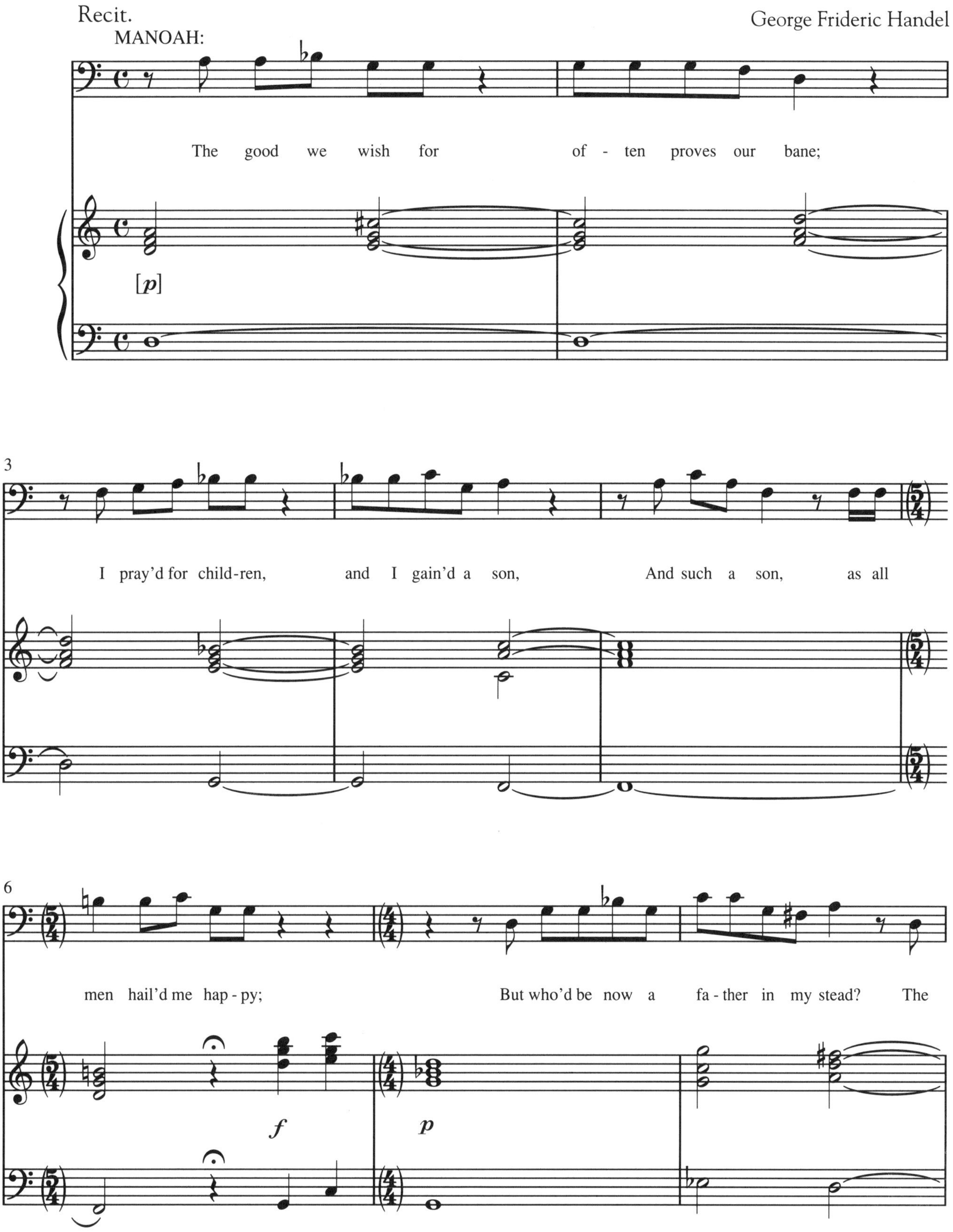

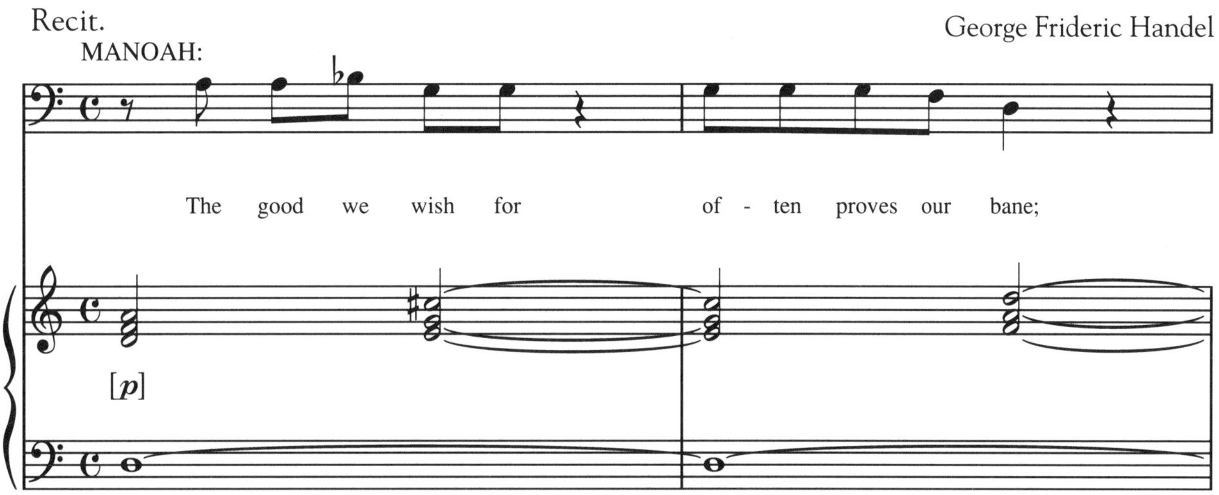

Recit.
MANOAH:
The good we wish for of - ten proves our bane;
[p]
3
I pray'd for child-ren, and I gain'd a son, And such a son, as all
6
men hail'd me hap - py;
But who'd be now a fa - ther in my stead? The
f
p

9
bless-ing drew a scor-pion's tail be - hind: This plant, se-lect and sa - cred, for a while The
12
mir - a - cle of men, was in an hour Ens-nar'd, as - sault-ed, ov-er-come, led
f
15
bound, His foes' de - ri - sion, Cap - tive, poor and blind.
p
Aria
Allegro
f
tr

Thy glo - rious deeds in - spir'd my tongue, Whilst
airs of joy from thence did flow, whilst airs of joy from thence did flow,

19
whilst
22
airs of joy
25
from thence did flow,
28
Thy glo - rious deeds, thy

31
glo - rious deeds in - spir'd my tongue, thy glo - rious deeds in -
34
spir'd my tongue, Whilst airs of joy from thence did flow,
37
whilst airs of joy
41

44
from thence did flow,
47
50
Thy glo - rious deeds in - spir'd my tongue, Whilst airs of joy from
54
thence did flow;
tr
tr

57
tr
61
Largo
p
To sor - rows now I tune my song,
p
66
And set my harp to notes of woe,
To sor - rows now I
72
tune my song, And set my harp to

78

notes __ of woe, __ to notes __ of woe, __ to

84

notes __ of woe, __ and set __ my harp __ to

89

Adagio

notes __ of woe, __ and set my harp __ to notes __ of woe. ____

95

Honor and arms
from
SAMSON

George Frideric Handel

16
such a foe,
Though I could end thee at a blow,
19
though I could end thee at a blow,
though I could end thee at a blow,
23
Poor vic - to - ry,
to con - quer thee,
Or
27
glo - - - - - - ry in thy

31
o - ver-throw!
f
35
Hon - or and arms scorn such a foe, scorn
p
39
such a foe, Though I could end thee at a blow, though I could
42
end thee at a blow, Poor vic - to - ry, to con - quer thee, poor vic - to-ry,

46

to con - quer thee, Or glo - - ry, or glo -

50

- - - ry in thy ov - er - throw, or

f

54

glo - ry, or glo - ry, or glo -

p

57

- - ry in thy o - ver - throw!

61
64
Fine
68
Van - quish a slave that is half slain! So mean a tri - umph I dis-dain, so
72
mean a tri - umph I dis-dain, I dis-dain,
76
Van-quish a slave that is half slain! So mean a tri - umph

*Fermata on Fine

80
I dis-dain,
I dis - dain, I dis-dain,
84
so mean a tri - umph,
so mean a tri - umph
p
88
I dis-dain,
so mean a tri - umph
I dis-dain.
f
92
Dal Segno al Fine

Schon eilet froh der Akkermann

(With joy th'impatient husbandman)

from

DIE JAHRESZEITEN

(The Seasons)

Franz Joseph Haydn

Aria

Allegretto
f
4
8
Schon - ei - let froh der Ak - ker-mann zur Ar - beit auf das
With joy th'im - pa - tient hus - band-man Drives forth his lus - ty
p.
12
Feld, in lan - gen Fur - chen schrie - tet er dem Pflu - ge flö - tend
team To where the well - us'd plough re-mains, Now loos - en'd from the

16
nach.
frost,
ten.
20
Schon ei - let froh der Ak - ker-mann zur Ar - beit auf das
With joy th'im - pa - tient hus - band-man Drives forth his lus - ty
ten.
ten.
24
Feld, in lan - gen Fur - chen
team To where the well - us'd
ten.
28
schrei - tet er dem Pflu - ge flö - tend nach, in lan - gen Fur - chen
plough re - mains, Now loos - en'd from the frost; To where the well - us'd

32
schrei - tet er dem Pflu - ge flö - tend nach,
plough re - mains, Now loos - en'd from the frost;
36
in lan - gen Fur - chen schrei - tet er dem Pflu - ge flö - tend
To where the well - us'd plough re - mains, Now loos - en'd from the
40
nach, in lan - gen Fur - chen schrei - tet er dem Pflu - ge flö - tend
frost; To where the well - us'd plough re - mains, Now loos - en'd from the
44
nach, flö - tend nach, flö - tend, flö - tend, flö - tend
frost, Now loos - en'd from the frost, from the

48
nach.
frost.
52
In ab - ge - mess - nem Gan - ge dann, in ab - ge - mess - nem
With mea - sur'd step he throws the grain, with mea - sur'd step he
56
Gan - ge dann wirft er den Sa - men aus,
throws the grain with in the boun-teous earth.
60
den birgt der Ak - ker treu, den birgt der
O sun, soft show'rs and dews! O sun, soft

64
Ak - ker treu und reift ihn bald zur gold' - nen
show'rs and dews! The gold - en ears in plen - ty
68
Frucht, und reift
bring; The gold - -
sempre p
72
76
ihn bald zur
- en ears in plen - ty, in

80
opt.
gold' - nen Frucht. In
plen - ty bring! With
f
84
ab - ge - mess - nem Gan - ge dann, in ab - ge - mess - nem Gan - ge dann wirft
mea - sur'd step he throws the grain, With mea - sur'd step he throws the grain with -
p
88
er den Sa - men aus, den
in the boun - teous earth. O
f
p
92
birgt der Ak - ker treu und reift ihn
sun, soft show'rs and dews! The gold - en

96
bald, ihn bald zur gold' - nen Frucht.
ears in plen - ty, in plen - ty bring!
cresc.
f
100
Schon
With
fz
fz
fz
104
ei - let froh der Ak - ker-mann zur Ar - beit auf das Feld, in
joy th'im - pa - tient hus - band-man Drives forth his lus - ty team To
p
108
lan - gen Fur - chen schrei - tet er dem Pflu - ge flö - tend nach,
where the well - us'd plough re-mains, Now loos - en'd from the frost,

112
in lan - gen _ Fur - chen _ schrei - tet _ er dem
And they _ their _ won - ted _ toil _ be - gin, Made
116
Pflu - ge flö - tend nach, in lan - gen _ Fur - chen _ schrei - tet er dem
cheer - ful by a song, And they _ their _ won - ted _ toil be - gin, Made
120
Pflu - ge flö - tend nach, in
cheer - ful by a song, And
pp
124
lan - gen _ Fur - chen _ schrei - tet _ er dem Pflu - ge flö - tend nach, in
they _ their _ won - ted _ toil _ be - gin, Made cheer - ful by a song, and

128
lan - gen Fur - chen schrei - tet er dem Pflu - ge flö - tend nach,
they their won - ted toil be - gin, Made cheer - ful by a song,
132
flö - tend nach, flö - tend, flö - tend, flö - tend nach,
made cheer - ful by a song, by a song,
p
p
136
flö - tend nach, flö - tend nach.
by a song, by a song.
pp
140

Erblikke hier, betörter Mensch

(In this, O vain, misguided man)

from

DIE JAHRESZEITEN

(The Seasons)

Franz Joseph Haydn

9
stum - mer Schreck - en drückt den gan - zen Um - fang der Na - tur.
vast ex - tend - ed waste In - wrapt in si - lent gloom.
p
Aria
Largo
Er-
In
p
fz
p
p
f
5
blik - ke hier, be - tör - ter Mensch, er - blik - ke dei - nes Le - bens Bild! Ver -
this O vain mis-guid-ed man, The pic - ture true of life be - hold! Soon
ten.
p
fz
p
pp

9
blü - het ist dein kur - zer Lenz, er - schöp - fet dei - nes Som - mers
pass thy hours of bloom-ing Spring, Thy Sum - mer-strength a - non de -
ten.
12
Kraft, er - schöp-fet dei - nes Som - mers Kraft.
clines, Thy Sum - mer strength a - non de - clines;
p
15
Schon welkt dein Herbst dem Al-ter zu, schon
Then comes the Au - tumn of thy days, And
p

18
fz
naht der blei - che Win - ter sich und
Win - ter last, with drea - ry close, Meet
20
zei - get dir das off - ne
em - blem of the yawn - ing
22
Grab. Schon naht der blei - che
tomb, And Win - ter last with

24
Win - ter sich und zei - get dir das
drea - ry close, Meet em - blem of the
ten.
26
Allegro molto (𝅗𝅥 = 92)
off - ne Grab.
yawn - ing tomb;
p
p
ff
30
Wo sind sie nun, die hoh'n Ent - wür - fe,
Where now are fled thy lof - ty schemes,
3
p
f

35
die Hoff - nun - gen vom
Thy flat - t'ring hopes of
p
40
Glück,
wealth,
3
die Sucht
Thy long -
45
nach eit - lem Ruh - me,
- ings af - ter fame,
der Sor - gen schwe - re
And all thy world - ly
f
p

50
Last?
cares?
Wo sind sie nun, die Won - ne -
Where now are fled the mirth - ful
fz
p
pp
56
ta - ver - schwelgt in Üp - pig - keit?
days, In wan - ton plea - sure past?
61
Wo sind sie nun, die Won - ne - ta - ge,
Where now are fled the mirth - ful days,
f

68
ver - schwelgt in Üp - pig - keit?
In wan - ton plea-sure past?
Und
And
fz
fz
fz
3
fz
74
wo, und wo die fro - hen_ Näch - te, im Tau -
where, a - las! those fes - tive_ nights, In gid -
p
fz
p
81
- mel durch-ge - wacht? und wo die fro - hen
- dy rev - els spent? And where those fes - tive
f
pp

88
Näch - te, im Tau - mel durch - ge - wacht? Wo sind sie nun?
nights, In gid - dy rev - els spent? Where, where, a - las!
f
f
94
wo?
where?
Ver-schwun - den sind sie
All van - ish'd, van-ish'd
f
p
101
wie ein Traum. Nur Tug - end bleibt.
like a dream. For nought but truth re - mains.
f

Rollend in schäumenden Wellen

(Rolling in foaming billows)
from
DIE SCHÖPFUNG
(The Creation)

Franz Joseph Haydn

Recit.
RAPHAEL:
Und Gott sprach: Es samm-le sich das Was-ser un - ter dem Him - mel zu - sam-men an
And God said, Let the wa - ters un - der the heav - en be gath-er - ed to - geth - er to
p
4
ei - nem Platz, und es er - schei-ne das trock-ne Land; und es ward so. Und Gott nann-te das trock-ne
one place, and let the dry land ap-pear: and it was so. And God call-ed the dry land
8
Land: Er-de, und die Samm - lung der Was-ser nann-te er Meer, und Gott sah, dass es gut war.
earth, and the gath - er-ing of wa-ters call-ed he seas: and God saw that it was good.
f

Allegro assai
f

3
p

5
f

7
p
f

9

11
13
Rol - lend in schäu - men - den
Roll - ing in foam - ing
p
15
Wel - len be - wegt sich un - ges-tüm das
bil - lows, Up - lift - ed, roars the boist' - rous
18
Meer. Rol - lend in schäu men-den Wel - len be -
sea. Roll - ing in foam - ing bil - lows, Up -
fz
p
fz
p

21
wegt sich, be - wegt sich un - ges-tüm das
lift - ed, up - lift - ed, roars the bois - t'rous
24
Meer, be - wegt sich un - ges-tüm das Meer.
sea, up - lift - ed roars the bois - t'rous sea.
f
27
Hü - gel und Fel - sen er - schei - nen, der Ber - ge
Moun-tains and rocks _ now e - merge, Their tops a -
p
31
Gip - fil steigt em - por, der Ber - ge Gip - fel steigt em-
mong the clouds as - cend, their tops a - mong the clouds as-

35
por.
cend.
Hü - gel und Fel - sen er - schei - nen,
Moun-tains and rocks now e - merge,
der Ber - ge Gip - fel
Their tops a - mong the
f
p
39
steigt em - por, der Ber - ge Gip - fel steigt em - por, der Ber - ge
clouds as - cend, their tops a - mong the clouds as - cend, a - mong the
43
Gip - fel steigt em - por.
clouds their tops as - cend.
f
47
Die Flä - che,
Thro' th'o - pen
p

51
weit ge - dehnt, durch - läuft der brei - te
plains out - stretch - ing wide, In ser - pent
54
Strom in man - cher Krüm - me. Die Flä - che weit ge -
er - ror ri - vers flow. Thro' th'o - pen plains out -
58
dehnt, durch - läuft der brei - te Strom
stretch - ing wide, out - stretch - ing wide,
61
in man - cher Krüm-me, durch - läuft
In ser - pent er - ror, In ser - -

65

der brei - te Strom
- pent_ er - ror ri - vers *flow,*

68

in man-cher Krüm - - me.
ri - vers flow.

71

♩ = 80

f *p*

Lei - se
Soft - ly

3

76

rau - schend_ glei - tet fort im
purl - ing,_ glides on Thro'

79
stil - len Tal der hel - le Bach:
si - lent vales the lim - pid brook,
83
lei - se rau - schend glei -
Soft - ly purl - ing, glides
87
- tet fort im stil -
on Thro' si -
3
3
pp
90
- len Tal der hel - le Bach.
- lent vales the lim - pid brook,
3
3
3
3

94
Lei - se rau - schend
Soft - ly purl - ing,
97
glei - tet fort im stil - len
glides on Thro' si - lent
100
Tal der hel - le Bach;
vales the lim - pid brook,
103
lei - se rau - schend
Soft - ly purl - ing,

106
glei - - tet fort im stil -
glides on Thro' si -
pp
110
- len Tal der hel - le Bach,
- lent vales the lim - pid brook,
p
114
im stil - len Tal der
Thro' si - lent vales the
118
hel - le Bach.
lim - pid brook.
pp

Nun scheint in vollem Glanze der Himmel

(Now heav'n in fullest glory shone)

from

DIE SCHÖPFUNG

(The Creation)

Recit.

Franz Joseph Haydn

12
steht der Lö-we da.
stands the taw-ny li-on.
tr
tr
Presto
16
Hier schiesst der ge-len - ki - ge Ti-ger em-por.
With sud - den leap the flex-i-ble ti-ger ap-pears.
3
3
f
19
Presto (♩. = 112)
24
Das zack-'ge Haupt er -
The nim-ble stag bears
simile

27
hebt der schnel - le Hirsch.
up his branch-ing head.
simile
31
Mit flie-gen-der Mäh-ne springt und
Withfly - ing mane, and fie - ry
36
wieh'rt voll Mut und Kraft das ed - le Ross.
look, im - pa - tient neighs the no - ble steed.
40
Andante (♪ = 120)
p
Auf
The

44
grü - nen Mat-ten wei-det schon das Rind, in Heer-den ab - ge - teilt.
cat-tle in herds al - rea - dy seek their food On fields and mea-dows green.
p
p
48
Die Trif-ten deckt, als wie ge - sät, das wol-len-
And o'er the ground, as plants, are spread The flee - cy,
p
53
rie-che, sanf-te Schaf. Wie Staub ver - brei - tet sich in Schwarm und
meek, and bleat-ing flocks. Un - num-ber'd as the sands in swarms a -
p
56
Adagio (♪ = 88)
Wir - bel das Heer der In-sek-ten.
rose The host of in-sects.

60
a tempo
In lan - gen Zü - gen kriecht am Bo - den das Ge - würm.
In long di - men-sion creeps, with sin - uous trace, the worm.
fz
p a tempo
Aria
Maestoso (♩ = 84)
f
fz
fz
fz
6
p
11
Nun scheint in vol - lem Glan - ze der Him-mel.
Now heav'n in full - est glo - ry shone;
f

16
Nun prangt in ih - rem Schmuk - ke die
Earth smil'd in all her rich at -
p
20
Er - de.
tire,
f
fz
fz
24
Die Luft er -
The room of
fz
p
28
füllt das leich - te Ge - fie der,
air with fowl is fill'd,
die
The

32
Was - ser schwellt der Fi - sche Ge - wim - mel;
wa - ter swell'd by shoals of fish;
36
den Bo - den drückt der Tie - re
By heav - y beasts the ground is
40
Last, den Bo - den drückt der
trod, By heav - y beasts the
44
Tie - re Last.
ground is trod;
fz
f
fz
sf

48
Doch war noch Al - les nicht voll-
But all the work was not com-
fz
fz
p
52
bracht, doch war noch al - les nicht voll - bracht.
plete, But all the work was not com - plete;
Dem Gan - zen
There want - ed
f
p
57
fehl - te das Ge - schöpf, das Got - tes Wer - ke
yet that won-drous be - ing, That grate - ful should God's
p
p
61
dank - bar seh'n, des
pow'r ad - mire, With
f

65
Her - ren Gü - te prei - sen soll.
heart and voice his good - ness praise.
p
f
69
Doch war noch Al - les nicht voll - bracht. Dem Gan-zen
But all the work was not com - plete; There want-ed
p
73
fehl - te das Ge - schöpf, das Got - tes Wer - ke
yet that won - drous be - ing, That grate - ful should God's
p
77
dank - bar seh'n, des Her - ren Gü - te
pow'r ad - mire, With heart and voice his
3
pp

81
prei - sen _ soll, das
good - ness _ praise, That
f
p
85
Got - tes Wer - ke dank - bar seh'n, des Her - ren
grate - ful should _ God's powr ad - mire, With heart and
89
Gü - te prei - - sen _ soll, des Her - ren
voice, With heart, _ With heart and
f
93
Gü - te _ prei - - sen _ soll,
voice _ his _ good - ness _ praise,
f

97

des Her - ren Gü - te, des
With heart and voice, ______ With

p

100

Her - ren Gü - te ______ prei - sen ___ soll.
heart and voice his ______ good - ness ___ praise.

3

pp

f

104

fz

fz

Is not his word like a fire?

(Ist nicht des Herrn Wort wie ein Feuer?)

from

ELIJAH

Felix Mendelssohn

10
ham - mer that break - eth the rock, that break - eth the rock in - to
Ham - mer, der Fel - sen zer - schlägt? der Fel - sen, der Fel - sen zer -
p
[p]
13
piec - es? like a fire, like a fire, and like a
schlägt? wie ein Ham - mer, wie ein
p
16
ham - mer that break - eth, that break - eth the
Ham - mer, ein Ham - mer, der Fel - sen zer -
f
sf
cresc.
19
rock. His word is like a fire, and like a
schlägt? sein Wort ist wie ein Feu - er und wie ein
f
p
[pp]

22
ham - mer, a ham - mer that break - eth the
Ham - mer, ein Ham - mer, der Fel - sen zer -
[cresc.]
25
rock.
schlägt.
For God is
Gott ist ein
28
an - gry, an - gry with the wick-ed ev-'ry day, for God is
rech - ter Rich - ter, und ein Gott der täg-lich droht; ein rech - ter
33
an - gry with the wick-ed ev-'ry day; and if the wick-ed
Rich - ter, und ein Gott der täg-lich droht; will man sich nicht be -

37
cresc.
turn not; the Lord will whet his sword, will whet his
keh - ren, so hat er sein Schwert ge - wetzt, sein Schwert ge -
41
f
f
sword; and He hath bent his bow, and
wertzt, und sei - nen Bo - gen ge - spannt, und
cresc.
f
44
made it rea - dy, and made it rea - dy,
zie - let, zie - let,
f
ff
48
[sf]
f
rea - dy! Is not his word like a
zie - let! Ist nicht des Herrn Wort wie ein
fp
[p]
p

51
fire?
Feu - er?
and like a
und wie ein
ff
p
54
ham - mer that break - eth the rock, and like a ham - mer that break - eth the rock; is not his
Ham - mer, der Fel - sen zer-schlägt, und wie ein Ham - mer, der Fel - sen zer-schlägt, und wie ein
[sempre p]
pp
58
word like a fire, and like a ham - mer, a
Ham - - mer, wie ein Ham - mer, ein
61
ham - mer that break - eth the rock? that
Ham - mer, der Fel - sen zer - schlägt, der
cresc.
f

64
break - eth the rock, that break - eth the
Fel - sen zer - schlägt, zer - schlägt,
p
67
rock; and like a fire, like a ham - mer that
und wie ein Ham - mer, ein Ham - mer der
cresc.
70
break - eth the rock; is not his word like a
Fel - sen zer - schlägt. Ist nicht sein Wort wie ein
p
73
ham - mer that break - eth the rock, is not his
Ham - mer, der Fel - sen zer - schlägt. Ist nicht sein

76
word like a ham - mer that break - eth,
Wort wie ein Ham - mer, der Fel - sen,
cresc.
cresc.
Più lento
79
the rock in - to piec - es?
Fel - sen zer - schlägt?
Is not his
Ist nicht des
ff
f
83
word like a ham - mer that break - eth the rock?
Herrn Wort wie ein Ham - mer, der Fel - sen zer-schlägt?
Tempo Primo
f
ff
87

Lord God of Abraham
(Herr Gott Abrahams)
from
ELIJAH

Felix Mendelssohn

13
cresc.
I - saac, and Is - ra - el; this day let it be known that Thou art God, and I am thy ser - vant!
I - saaks und I - sra-els, lass heut kund wer - den, dass du Gott bist, und ich dein Knecht!
cresc.
17
f
dim.
cresc.
Lord God of A - bra - ham! O show to all this peo - ple that I have done these things
Herr Gott A - bra - hams! und dass ich sol - ches Al - les nach dei - nem Wor - te ge - than,
f dim. p [dim. p]
p
cresc.
sf
21
dim.
ac - cord - ing to thy word! O hear me, Lord, and an - swer me, O hear me,
nach dei - nem Wor - te ge - than. Er - hö - re mich Herr, er - hö - re mich! er - hö - re mich
dim.
p

25
cresc.
ff
Lord, and an - swer me!
Herr, er - hö - re mich!
Lord God of A - bra-ham,
Herr Gott A - bra-hams,
cresc.
ff
28
p
cresc.
sf
I - saac, and Is - ra - el; O hear me, O hear me and an - swer me; and
I - saaks und I - sra-els, er - hö - re mich Herr, er - hö - re mich! dass
p
cresc.
f
31
show this peo - ple that Thou art Lord God; and let their hearts a - gain be
dies Volk wis - se, dass du Herr Gott bist, dass du ihr Herz da-nach be -
p
p

34
cresc.
dim.
turn - ed; O show this peo - ple that Thou art Lord God, and
keh rest! dass dies Volk wis - se, dass du Herr Gott bist, dass
cresc.
p
37
let their hearts a - gain be turn - ed, Lord;
du ihr Herz da - nach be - keh - rest. Herr,
mf
mf
40
and let their hearts, and let their hearts a - gain be turn - ed!
dass du ihr Herz, dass du ihr Herz da - nach be - keh - rest.
p
pp
pp

It is enough!

(Es ist genug!)

from

ELIJAH

Felix Mendelssohn

14
I am not bet - ter than my fa - thers. It is e - nough!
ich bin nicht bes - ser denn mei - ne Vä - ter. Es ist ge - nug!
19
cresc.
it is e - nough! Now take a - way my life, I am not
es ist ge - nug! So nimm nun mei - ne See - le, ich bin nicht
cresc.
sf
p
23
cresc.
bet - ter, not bet - ter than my fa - thers, I am not bet - ter, I am not
bes - ser, nicht bes - ser denn mei - ne Vä - ter, ich bin nicht bes - ser, denn mei - ne
p

28
dim.
bet - ter than my fa - thers.
Vä - ter, denn mei - ne Vä - ter.
sf
p
cresc.
dim.
p
33
I de - sire to live no long - er: now let me die, for my
Ich be - geh - re nicht mehr zu le - ben, denn mei - ne Ta - ge sind ver -
pp
38
sf
cresc.
days are but van - i - ty, now let me die, for my days are but
geb - lich ge - we - sen; denn mei - ne Ta - ge sind ver - geb - lich, ver -
sf
p
poco a

43
sf
van - i-ty, but van - i - ty!
geb - lich ge - we - sen.
poco
cresc.
al
al
46
Molto allegro vivace 𝅗𝅥 = 92
f
I have been ve-ry jeal - ous for the
Ich ha - be ge - ei - fert um den
ff
f
[sf]
50
Lord, for the Lord God of Hosts, for the child - ren of
Herrn, un den Gott Ze - ba - oth, denn die Kin - der
ff
p
[sf]

55
sf
sf
Is - ra - el have bro - ken thy cov-e-nant, bro - ken thy
I - sra - els ha - ben dei - nen Bund ver - las - sen, die - nen Bund ver -
ff
sf
60
co-ve-nant, have bro - ken thy cov - e - nant, and thrown down thine al - tars, and
las - sen und dei - ne Al - tä - re ha - ben sie zer - bro - chen, und
p
65
slain all thy proph - ets, slain them with the sword, and slain thy
dei - ne Pro - phe - ten mit dem Schwert er - würgt, und dei - ne Pro -
p
sf
p

70
proph - ets, slain them with the sword.
phe - ten mit dem Schwert er-würgt.
I have been ve-ry
Ich ha - be ge-
75
jeal - ous for the Lord,
ei - fert um den Herrn,
for the Lord God of
um den Gott Ze - ba-
80
Hosts, ve-ry jeal-ous for the Lord, the Lord God of Hosts, and I, e - ven
oth, ge - ei-fert um den Herrn, den Gott Ze-ba-oth. Und ich bin al-

86
p
cresc.
I on - ly am left; and they seek my life, and they seek my
lein ü - brig ge - blie - ben; und sie steh'n da - nach dass sie mir, mein
pp
92
sf
life to take it, to take it a -
Le - ben neh - men, mein Le - ben
cresc.
96
ff
Adagio ♩ = 66
con forza
dim.
way! It is e - nough, it is e -
neh - men! Es ist ge - nug, es ist ge -
ff
sf

101

p

nough! It is e - nough, O Lord, now take a-way my

nug! Es ist ge - nug, so nimm nun Herr _ mei - ne

p

106

life, __ for I am not bet - ter than my fa - thers! Now let me

See - le, ich bin nicht bes - ser denn mei-ne Vä - ter. Nimm nun, o

p

112

cresc. *dim.* *pp*

die, Lord, ____________ take a - way __ my life! __

Herr, nimm, ____________ nimm, o Herr, mei - ne See - le!

cresc.

For the mountains shall depart

(Ja, es sollen wohl Berge weichen)

from

ELIJAH

Felix Mendelssohn

9
p
glad, my glo - ry re - joi - ceth, and my flesh shall al - so rest in hope.
Herz und ich bin fröh - lich; auch mein Fleisch wird si - cher lie - gen.
[Aria] sostenuto assai (♩ = 100)
11
p
14
p
For the moun - tains shall de - part, and the hills, the
Ja, es sol - len wohl Ber - ge wei - chen, Ber - ge wei - chen und
dim.
p
18
hills be re - mov - ed; but thy kind - ness shall not de - part;
Hü - gel hin - fal - len, a - ber dei - ne Gna - de,
cresc.

21
but thy kind - ness, thy kind - ness shall not de -
a - ber dei - ne Gna - de, dei - ne Gna - de wird nicht von mir
p
cresc.
dim.
24
part from me; nei - ther shall the co - ve - nant of thy
wei - chen, und der Bund dei - nes Frie - dens soll nicht
p
p
27
peace, of thy peace be re - mov - ed, nei - ther shall the
fal - len, und der Bund er soll nicht fal - len, und der Bund dei - nes
cresc.
p
cresc.
sf
31
co - ve-nant of thy peace be re - mov - ed; but thy kind-ness shall not de -
Frie - dens, dei - nes Frie - dens soll nicht fal - len. Dei - ne Gna - de wird nicht von mir
dim.
p

35
cresc.
part, shall not de - part,
wei - chen, wird nicht von mir wei - chen!
but thy kind - ness shall not de -
Dei - ne Gna - de wird nicht von mir
cresc.
p
39
part, shall not de - part from me; nei - ther shall be re -
wei - chen, nicht von mir wei - chen und der Bund
p
43
mov - ed the co - ve - nant of thy peace.
dei - nes Frei - dens soll nicht fal - len.
p

Gott sei mir gnädig
(O God, have mercy)
from
PAULUS
(St. Paul)

Felix Mendelssohn

10
gros - sen Barm-her - zig - keit, nach dei-ner gros - sen Barm-her - zig -
to Thy lov - ing kind - ness, yea, e-ven for mer - cy's
13
keit. Ver-wirf mich nicht. ver-wirf mich nicht von dei - nem
sake. De-ny me not, O cast me not a - way from
p
16
An-ge-sicht und nimm dei-nen hei-li-gen Geist nicht von mir, und nimm dei-nen hei-li-gen Geist nicht von
Thy pres-ence, and take not Thy spi-rit from me, O Lord, and take not Thy spir-it from me, O
sf
p

19

mir, und nimm ______ dei - nen hei - li - gen Geist nicht von
Lord, o take ______ not ______ Thy spir - it from me, O

p

22

mir. Ein ge - äng - ste - tes und zer -
Lord. Lord, a bro - ken heart, and a

sf *sf* *p*

ten.

p

25

schla - ge - nes Herz wirst du Gott nicht ver - ach - ten, ein ge - äng - ste - tes
con - trite heart is of - fer'd be - fore Thee; Lord, a bro - ken heart,

cresc.

28 und zer-schla - ge-nes Herz wirst du Gott nicht ver - ach - ten. Gott sei mir

and a con - trite heart is of - fer'd be - fore Thee. O God, have

f

ten.

p

31 gnä - dig nach dei - ner Gü - te, nach dei - ner gros - sen Barm-her - zig -

mer - cy, have mer - cy up - on me, ac - cord-ing to Thy lov - ing kind -

dim.

f *p*

34 keit, nach dei - ner gros - sen Barm-her - zig - keit.

ness, yea, e - ven for Thy mer - cy's sake.

sf

37 *f* *p* *dim.*

40
Allegro maestoso (𝅗𝅥 = 100)
quasi Recit.
Denn ich will die Ue - ber - tre - ter dei - ne We - ge
I will speak of Thy sal - va - tion, I will teach trans -
f
sf
43
leh - ren, dass sich die Sün - der zu dir be - keh - ren, dass sich die Sün - der zu
gres - sors, and sin-ners shall be con-ver - ted un - to Thee, shall be con - ver - ted, con -
f
47
dir be - keh - ren.
ver - ted un - to Thee.
Denn ich will die Ue - ber -
I will speak of Thy sal -
sf
50
tre - ter dei - ne We - ge leh - ren, dass sich die Sün - der zu dir be -
va - tion, and will teach trans - gres - sors, that all the sin - ners shall be con -
f

53
sf
keh - ren, dass sich die Sün - der zu dir be - keh - ren! Herr thu - e
ver - ted, shall be con - ver - ted, con - ver - ted un - to Thee; Then o - pen
p
58
mei - ne Lip - pen auf! Herr thu - e
Thou my Lips, o Lord! Then o - pen
f
p
62
mei - ne Lip - pen auf, dass mein Mund dei - nen Ruhm ver -
Thou my Lips, o Lord! and my mouth shall show forth Thy
f
p
66
ritard.
kün - di - ge, dass mein Mund dei - nen Ruhm ver - kün - di -
glo - rious praise, and my mouth shall show forth Thy glo - rious
ritard.

71
Adagio (Tempo I)
ge. Und til - ge mei - ne Sün - den nach dei - ner
praise! O blot out my trans - gres - sions, ac - cord - ing
pp
sf
p
75
gros - sen Barm - her - zig - keit, nach dei - ner gros - sen Barm - her - zig -
to Thy lov - ing kind - ness, yea, e - ven for Thy mer - cy's
78
keit. Herr! ver - wirf mich nicht, Herr!
sake, Lord! for Thy mer - cy's sake, Lord!
dim.
81
ver - wirf mich nicht!
for Thy mer - cy's sake!
pp

Crucifixus
from
MESSA DI GLORIA

Giacomo Puccini

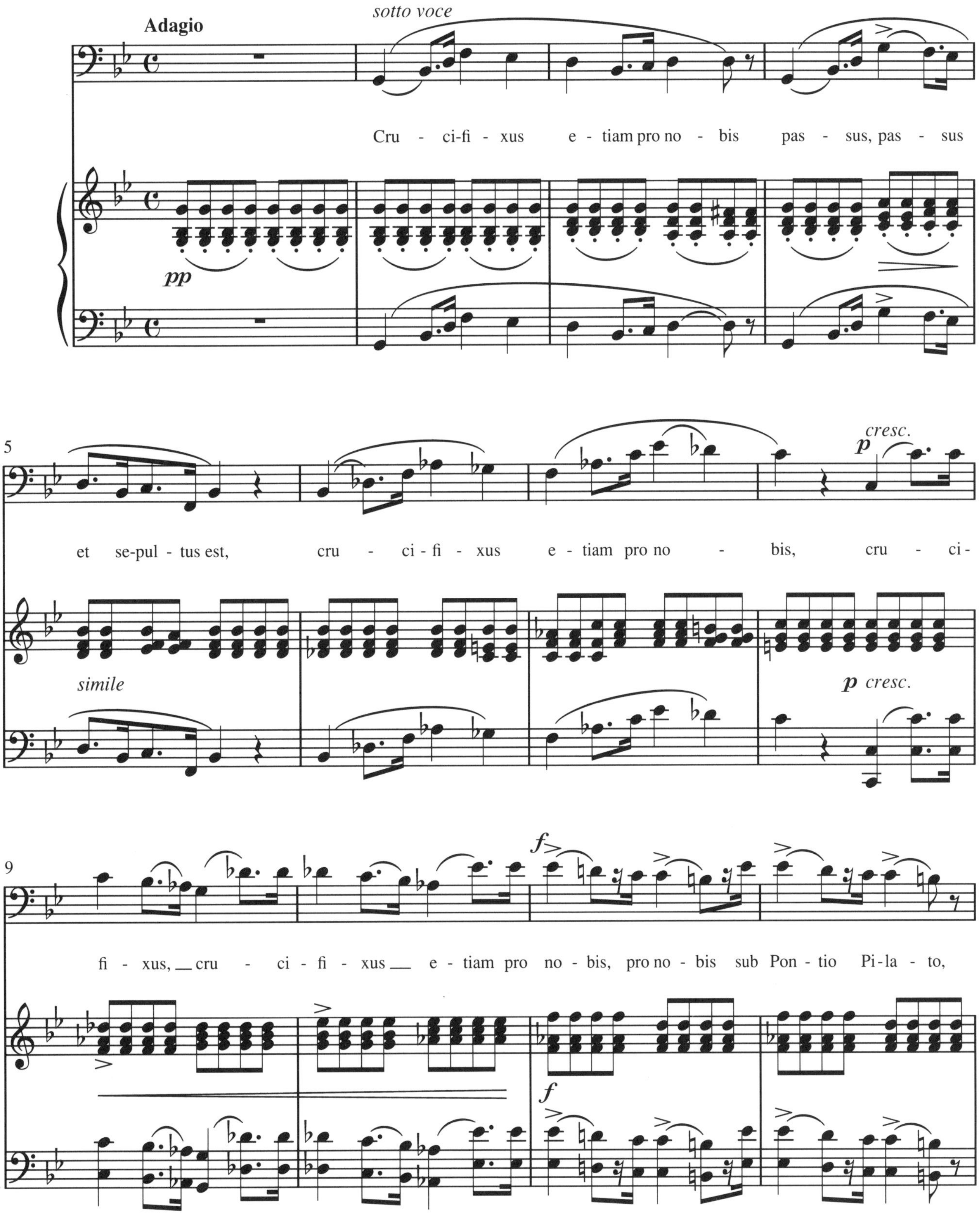
Adagio
sotto voce
Cru - ci-fi - xus e - tiam pro no - bis pas - sus, pas - sus
pp
5
et se-pul - tus est, cru - ci - fi - xus e - tiam pro no - bis, cru - ci -
cresc.
p
simile
p cresc.
9
fi - xus, cru - ci - fi - xus e - tiam pro no - bis, pro no - bis sub Pon - tio Pi - la - to,
f
f

13
pp
cru - ci-fi - xus e - tiam pro no - bis, e - tiam pro no -
3
pp
3
16
sotto voce
- bis.
Cru - ci-fi - xus
p
pp
19
e - tiam pro no - bis
pas - sus, pas - sus et se-pul - tus est.
22
cresc. e stringendo
Cru - ci-fi - xus, cru - ci-fi - xus, cru - ci-fi - xus
cresc. e stringendo

25
rall.
stent.
e - ti - am pro no - bis, pas - sus, pas - sus et se - pul - tus
rall.

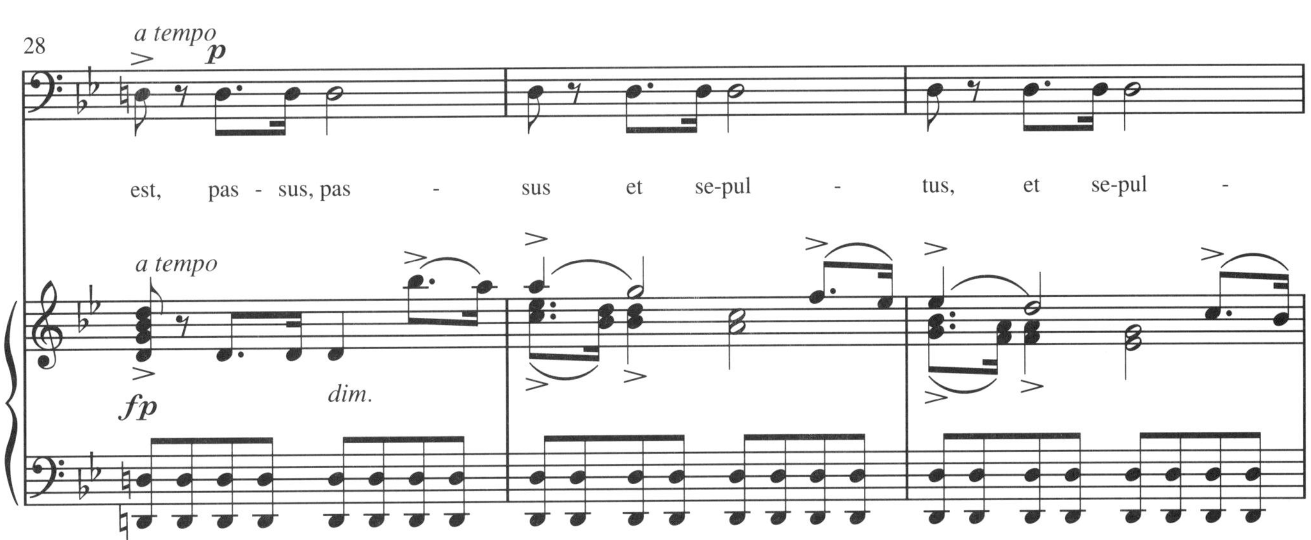
28
a tempo
est, pas - sus, pas - sus et se-pul - tus, et se-pul -
a tempo
dim.

31
tus, se-pul - tus est.

Pro peccatis
from
STABAT MATER

Gioachino Rossini

20
Je - sum in tor - men - tis, et fla - gel - lis
tr
ff
sf sf sf
25
tr
sub - di - tum.
pp
ff
ff
29
Pro pec - ca - tis su - æ gen - tis
3
pp
33
vi - dit Je - sum in tor - men - tis

37
et fla - gel - lis, et fla - gel - lis,
f
41
et fla - gel - lis sub - di -
pp
44
tum.
pp
sf
pp
48
pp

52
sf
ff
3
tr
55
Vi - dit
sotto voce.
59
su - um dul - cem na - tum mo - ri -
63
en - tem de - so - la - tum dum e -
tr
ff
sf
sf

67
mi - sit spi - ri - tum.
tr
pp
ff
sf
ff
72
Vi - dit su - um dul - cem na - tum
pp
76
mo - ri - en - tem de - so - la - tum
80
dum e - mi - sit, dum e - mi - sit,
f

84
dum e - mi - sit spi - ri - tum.
p
88
vi - dit su - um dul - cem na - tum,
92
mo - ri - en - tum de - so - la - tum
mf
tr
ff
96
dum e - mi - sit, dum e - mi - sit
sf
sf
pp

100
spi - ri - tum,
vi - dit su - um
p
104
dul - cem na - tum mo - ri - en - tem
mf
108
de - so - la - tum dum e - mi - sit,
tr
ff
sf
sf
sf
112
dum e - mi - sit spi - ri -
pp

115
tum, e - mi - sit, e - mi - sit
ff
118
spi - ri - tum, e - mi - sit,
121
e - mi - sit spi - ri - tum.
tr
124

Quoniam tu solus sanctus
from
MESSE SOLENNELLE

Gioachino Rossini

21
pp
ff
f
25
tr
ff
mf
f
ff
29
Quo - ni - am tu so - lus sanc - tus
pp
33
Quo - ni - am tu so - lus sanc - tus Tu
37
so - lus Do - mi-nus tu so - lus Do - mi-nus Tu
simile stacc.

41
so - lus al - tis - si-mus Je - su Chris - te
ff
ff
p
45
Je - su Je - su Chris - te Tu
mf
cresc.
ff
ff
f
49
so - lus Tu so - lus al - tis - si - mus al -
pp
f
f
53
tis - si - mus Je - su Chris - te Tu so - lus al-
ff
ff
fp

57
tis - si-mus Je - su Je - su Chris -
tr
f
ff
60
te
ff
f
pp
ff
64
Tu so - lus
f
pp
pp
tr
68
sanc - tus Tu so - lus Do - mi-nus Tu so - lus al -
simile stacc.
tr
tr

72
tis - si-mus tu so - lus al - tis - si - mus
cresc.
75
Je - su Chris-te
ff
tr
f
mf
ppp
79
Quo - ni-am tu so - lus tu so - lus sanc - tus Tu
83
so - lus Do - mi - nus Tu so - lus al - tis - si - mus
f

87
Je - su Chris - te Tu so - lus sanc - tus Tu
pp
ppp
91
so - lus Do - mi-nus Tu so - lus al - tis - si - mus
cresc.
95
Je - su Chris - te Je - su Chris - te
opt.
f
ff
pp
99
Tu so - lus Tu

102
so - lus
al - tis - si - mus
105
Je - su Chris - - te
ppp
f
f
109
mf
Tu so - lus tu so - lus al - tis - si-mus
f
pp
f
113
Al - tis - si - mus Je - su Chris -
f
ff

116
te
Tu
so
-
lus
al
-
tis
-
si
-
mus
ff
pp
119
tr
Je
-
su
Je
-
su
Chris
-
-
te
f
ff
ff
122
f
pp
ff
f
pp
127
Tu
so
-
lus
sanc
-
tus
Tu
so
-
lus
tr
tr
pp
simile stacc.

131

Do - mi-nus Tu so - lus al - tis - si-mus Tu so - lus al -

tr

cresc.

135

tis - si - mus Je - su ___ Chris-te

ff

tr

mf

139

Quo - ni-am Tu so - lus tu so - lus ___

ppp

143

cresc.

sanc - tus Tu so - lus ___ Do - mi - nus Tu so - lus al -

147
tis - si - mus Je - su Chris - te Tu so - lus
f
pp
pppp
151
sanc - tus Tu so - lus Do - mi-nus Tu so - lus al -
cresc.
155
tis - si-mus Je - su Chris - te Je - su Chris -
rinf.
f
ff
159
te Tu so - lus
pp
stacc.

162
Tu so - lus
Al -
165
tis - si - mus Je - su Chris - -
ppp
169
te
Tu so - lus tu so - lus Al -
f
f
f
pp
173
tis - si-mus
Al - tis - si - mus Je - su Chris -
f
f
ff

177
te
Tu
so
-
lus
al
-
tis
-
si - mus
ff
ff
fp
180
tr
Je
-
su
Je
-
su
Chris
-
te
Tu
so
-
lus
f
f
183
Je
-
su
Chris
-
te
Tu so
-
lus
ff
186
Je
-
su
Je
-
su
opt.
Chris
-
8va
fff
ff

189

te

193

ff

8va

197

ff

f

201

ff

pp

205

Confutatis
from
REQUIEM

Giuseppe Verdi

17
ci - nis, Ge - re cu - ram me - i fi - nis. O - ro
p
21
p
rall.
sup - plex et ac - cli - nis, Cor con - tri - tum qua - si ci - nis,
p
rall.
25
f
Ge - re, Ge - re cu - ram me - i fi -
28
ff
nis. Con - fu - ta - tis ma - le - dic - tis,
mf
ff

31
Flam - mis a - cri-bus ad - dic - tis,
mf
ff
p dolce cantabile
33
Vo - ca me cum be - ne - dic - tis,
p
37
Vo - ca me cum be - ne - dic - tis, Vo - ca me,
f
p
41
Vo-ca me cum be-ne - dic - tis.
f
pp

45
O - ro sup - plex et ac - cli - nis,
pp
48
Cor con - tri - tum qua - si ci - nis, Ge - re
52
p
cu - ram me - i fi - nis, O - ro sup - plex et ac - cli - nis, Cor con -
p
p
56
f
tri - tum qua - si ci - nis, Ge - re, Ge - re cu -
f

60
ram me - i fi - nis, Ge - - - - re, —
f
f
64
Ge - re — cu - ram — me - i fi - nis,
pp
pp
68
O - ro sup-plex et ac - cli - nis, Ge - re
poco rall.
poco rall.
71
cu - ram, — Ge - re cu-ram me - i fi - nis.
ten.
f
8va